Scc

WITHDRAWN

Collin College Library
SPRING CREEK CAMPUS
Plano, Texas 75074

HV   Darling, Rosalyn
1568   Benjamin.
D367
2013   Disability and
                 identity.

$55.00

Disability and Identity

Disability in Society

Ronald J. Berger, series editor

Disability and Identity

Negotiating Self in a Changing Society

Rosalyn Benjamin Darling

LYNNE
RIENNER
PUBLISHERS

BOULDER
LONDON

Published in the United States of America in 2013 by
Lynne Rienner Publishers, Inc.
1800 30th Street, Boulder, Colorado 80301
www.rienner.com

and in the United Kingdom by
Lynne Rienner Publishers, Inc.
3 Henrietta Street, Covent Garden, London WC2E 8LU

© 2013 by Lynne Rienner Publishers, Inc. All rights reserved

Library of Congress Cataloging-in-Publication Data
Darling, Rosalyn Benjamin.
  Disability and identity : negotiating self in a changing society / Rosalyn
Benjamin Darling.
    p. cm. — (Disability in society)
  Includes bibliographical references and index.
  ISBN 978-1-58826-864-8 (hbk. : alk. paper)
1. People with disabilities. 2. Group identity. 3. Sociology of disability.
  I. Title.
HV1568.D367 2013
  305.9'08—dc23

                                                          2012040764

British Cataloguing in Publication Data
A Cataloguing in Publication record for this book
is available from the British Library.

Printed and bound in the United States of America

The paper used in this publication meets the requirements
of the American National Standard for Permanence of
Paper for Printed Library Materials Z39.48-1992.

  5 4 3 2 1

For Evelyn, Isaac, and Eli

Contents

Tables and Figures

Tables

Figures

Acknowledgments

When I saw the call for proposals for books in this series, my first reaction was to ignore it. I had recently retired and moved and no longer had ready access to the resources of a university. However, I was intrigued by the idea of revisiting the subject of stigma and identity as the fiftieth anniversary of E. Goffman's *Stigma: Notes on the Management of Spoiled Identity* neared. As a result, I did not need much encouragement from Andrew Berzanskis, acquisitions editor at Lynne Rienner Publishers, to begin the project. Shortly after starting the book, I moved again and, thanks to a visiting scholar appointment at the University of North Carolina at Chapel Hill, I again had access to an excellent library. Many thanks to Howard Aldrich, chair of UNC's Sociology Department, for making the appointment process so easy.

This book is not a collaborative effort, unlike some of my other books, so I truly appreciated the comments from two anonymous reviewers who read the first draft of the manuscript. I especially want to thank Adrienne Asch, whose insights were very helpful. I modified some of my discussions about disability pride and disability activism as a result of her input.

The ideas in this book reflect the current state of my thinking on identity and disability, but are based on many years of interaction with colleagues in sociology and disability studies. Most of all, my colleague Alex Heckert at Indiana University of Pennsylvania made huge contributions to Chapters 7 and 8. His quantitative skills enabled me to test my ideas about disability identity, and this book would not have been possible without his help.

I am indebted as well to the editors at Lynne Rienner Publishers, Andrew Berzanskis and Lesli Brooks Athanasoulis, who made the writing and publishing process as painless as possible. In addition, Lynne Rienner made helpful suggestions about the title. This book is much better as a result of their contributions.

Finally, I want to thank my family. My ninety-eight-year-old mother, Lillian Haber, will no doubt be proud of her daughter's most recent publication. My husband, Jon, has been an unfailing source of support for more than forty-three years; everything I accomplish depends on his help and encouragement. My sons and daughters-in-law, Eric, Seth, Susan, and Karen, are always in my thoughts, as are my grandchildren, Evelyn, Isaac, and Eli. I love you all.

—*Rosalyn Benjamin Darling*

Disability and Identity

1

Introduction

People with disabilities constitute a significant portion of the population. According to the US Bureau of the Census, in 2010 18.7 percent of the noninstitutionalized US population had a disability, and the numbers increase with age (Brault 2012). Although so many people are affected, until fairly recently, most of the literature on this population viewed disability as a form of deviance from the ability and appearance norms of Western society. During the past several decades, newer views have reconceptualized disability as a normal form of human variation, much like race or gender. However, much conceptual variability continues to exist. How have the self-conceptions of this population been affected by the views of others in society over time? I address this question by exploring the interactions between people with disabilities and the societies in which they live.

Certainly not all disabilities are the same, and societal reactions vary greatly from one disability to another. Some disabilities are readily apparent, whereas others remain hidden unless those who have them choose to reveal them to others. Some disabilities are congenital, but others develop later in life, and disability tends to increase dramatically with aging. Clearly, a person with an impairment such as asthma or diabetes may experience some limitations in life activities but probably will not encounter the stigma and social exclusion experienced by an individual with cerebral palsy who uses a wheelchair and a speech synthesizer. Most sociological research on disability has focused on individuals with impairments that have significant social consequences, and who are likely to have incorporated

1

their disability into their self-definitions or identities. In this book, I am concerned with those individuals who have the kinds of disabilities that tend to be associated with differential treatment in a variety of social situations.

Sociologist Erving Goffman's *Stigma* (Goffman 1963), perhaps the most influential study of the interaction between societal views and the self-concepts of people with disabilities, is subtitled, *Notes on the Management of Spoiled Identity*. Goffman was writing at a time when prevailing views of disability were overwhelmingly negative. Consequently, he believed that individuals with disabilities needed to learn techniques to minimize their differences in order to be accepted in society. More recently, the concept of spoiled identity has been increasingly questioned and challenged. However, few empirical studies have directly measured the identities of the population of people with disabilities in society today. This book is my attempt to increase knowledge about this understudied area and suggest directions for further research.

The concept of disability identity has been receiving increased attention in recent literature, much of which has come from scholars in the humanities and has been based largely on the personal experiences of disabled individuals. Although this literature certainly broadens our knowledge of the disability experience and provides important insights into the self-views of members of this population, it does not tell us whether these views are representative of the population as a whole. Studies undertaken from a social science perspective are needed to address the diversity of disability identity in modern society. In this book I take such a perspective, relying especially on sociological theories, concepts, and empirical studies to explore the evolution of the concept of disability identity from Goffman's time to the present. This inquiry seems especially appropriate on the fiftieth anniversary of Goffman's seminal publication.

Overview of the Book

Much of the early literature on the self-conceptions of people with disabilities suggested that prevailing self-views were negative. This literature was commonly based on a psychoanalytic perspective that suggested that bodily aberrations would have negative consequences for psychological well-being. In Chapter 2 I show that some of the empirical work that attempted to verify this suggestion was methodologically flawed, yet these views persisted for many years.

Early sociological perspectives of the self-conceptions of people with disabilities also suggested that these individuals would view themselves negatively. These sociological ideas derived from the premise that self-conceptions develop in response to interactions in a society that holds negative views of disability. This position was most clearly presented in the work of Erving Goffman, and his concept of stigma dominated sociological studies of disability for many years. He argued that an individual seen as having attributes of disability would be "reduced in our minds from a whole and usual person to a tainted, discounted one" (Goffman 1963, 3). In Chapter 2 I review the literature on stigma as part of an overview of attitudes toward disability in society.

Much of the sociological literature linking stigma with low self-esteem has roots in the symbolic interactionist perspective in general and "looking-glass self" theory in particular. The concept of the looking-glass self originated in the work of Charles Horton Cooley (1964). This concept suggests that our self-definitions derive from the definitions that we encounter when interacting with others. The theory posits that positive definitions will be reflected in favorable self-views, whereas negative definitions will have the opposite effect. Consequently, stigmatization would be expected to result in negative self-definitions.

However, as I show in later chapters, not all individuals with disabilities view themselves negatively. The existence of positive self-definitions in a stigmatizing society does not necessarily invalidate the looking-glass self argument, though. Symbolic interaction theory also includes the concepts of reference groups and significant others. These concepts suggest that the larger society's views may be filtered through interactions in smaller groups. We are likely to pay particular attention to the definitions we receive from the people who are most important to us. G. Becker (1980), for example, found that membership in a close-knit deaf community protected the older people she studied from the negative definitions of deafness in the larger society. In Chapter 3 I review concepts from symbolic interaction theory that are useful in understanding the relationship between societal views and the self-concepts of individuals with disabilities.

For some individuals, their disability is the most salient component of their self-concept. For others, having a disability plays only a minor role in the way they view themselves. In some cases, other devalued statuses overshadow disabilities in self-definitions. For example, P. Devlieger and G. Albrecht (2000) found that, in a sample of poor African Americans, race and class were more important than disability in determining self-identity. Studies of women with disabilities (see, e.g., Thomas 1999a) have suggested that "double oppression" may magnify the salience of disability identity. In Chapter 4 I explore how the relationships between disability and other devalued group identities shape the development of self-concept.

Since the 1970s and 1980s, many people with disabilities have become empowered as the disability rights movement (DRM) has grown. A number of sociologists (e.g., Anspach 1979; Britt and Heise 2000) have suggested a link between identity politics and a more positive construction of the disabled self. In fact, more recent writings by disability activists and disability studies scholars have introduced the concept of disability pride (see, e.g., Swain and French 2000). In Chapter 5 I look more closely at this concept. The idea of disabilty pride has been associated with a shift in the literature from a medical model that views disability as a pathological condition to a social model (Oliver 1996; Swain and Cameron 1999) that views disability as a normal form of human diversity. The social model sees disability as a social construction rather than as an inherent biological condition. Various writers have noted parallels between positive constructions like disability pride and similar constructions, such as gay pride and black pride, among other minority groups.

Much of the writing on disability pride has been theoretical or polemical. The writers have assumed that positive self-identities among individuals with disabilities have been increasing along with the increasing popularity of the social model. However, not everyone has been exposed to the social model, and even those who have been exposed to the model may not espouse it. A number of years ago, I suggested a typology of orientations toward disability (Darling 2003) that included other disability identities in addition to pride. I explore the diversity of identities among individuals with disabilities in society today in Chapter 6.

Since the 1990s, the existence of a variety of disability identities has been tested empirically. C. J. Gill (1997) and H. D. Hahn and T. L. Belt (2004) have attempted to measure the existence of disability pride among activists. More recently, my colleague and I (2010a) developed and tested an instrument to measure the diversity of orientations to disability suggested by the typology described above. The results confirm the existence of a variety of disability identities in US society today. In Chapter 7 I look more closely at these studies and discuss the empirical evidence for the existence of various disability identities.

Perhaps the most important variable in determining whether individuals view their disabilities positively is the point in the lifespan at which the disability is acquired. My colleague Alex Heckert and I (2010b) found that individuals with lifelong disabilities were much more likely to have an identity of disability pride, whereas those who acquired their disabilities later in life had more negative views. I explore the relationship between identity and age, along with the related variable of age at disability acquisition, in Chapter 8. I also focus on disability orientation at two points in the life course: childhood/adolescence and old age.

Views of disability appear to be changing slowly in modern society. Older, stigma-based views seem to be giving way to newer, more positive views. However, negative views continue to exist and to influence the self-esteem of people with disabilities. Newer technologies allow for the prenatal diagnosis of many impairments, commonly resulting in pregnancy termination among those who view disability negatively. If many disabilities become rarer in the future, will the identities of those living with disability be affected? In Chapter 9 I address this question in addition to speculating about trends relating to disability identity development in the future.

In the next section I review the theoretical paradigms that will be used in this book, namely symbolic interactionism and its derivative, identity theory. I define key concepts from these paradigms, including self and identity, and introduce the concept of disability orientation, which is broader than those of self and identity and encompasses the related variables of model and role. Finally, I briefly discuss the meanings of impairment and disability, and explain their use in this book.

Conceptual Framework and Definitions of Key Concepts

Self, Identity, and Orientation

In the chapters that follow, I apply a sociological framework to explain the relationship between society and self-concept in individuals with disabilities. Specifically, the perspective that will be used will be symbolic interactionism, the sociologically-based social psychology that originated in the work of G. H. Mead (1934), H. Blumer (1962), and others. Its basic premise is that individual attributes such as thought and self-concept derive from the individual's interactions in society. These interactions occur through language, or through shared meanings that enable a person to understand and respond to ideas expressed by others.

The mechanism through which interaction occurs is "taking the role of the other" (Mead 1934) or "role-taking," the process of understanding and internalizing the messages one receives in the course of interaction. Shared language makes role-taking possible. The symbolic interactionist view of the self begins with the premise that individuals receive definitions of themselves in the course of interacting with others. Through the mechanism of role-taking, they understand and internalize these definitions, incorporating them into their beliefs about themselves. For example, a student who receives positive feedback in the form of good grades and praise from teachers is likely to think of himself or herself as a good student. Over the years, many studies have explored the nature of the process of internalization and have shown that not all definitions have equal weight in determining a person's self-concept; however, the general association between the appraisals of others and self-appraisals has been supported (Lundgren 2004).

This book is about the self-concepts of people with disabilities. I use the terms *self, self-concept, self-view,* and *self-definition* interchangeably to refer to how people think about themselves. M. H. Kuhn and T. S. McPartland (1954) have noted that self-definitions include both "consensual," or fixed, attributes, such as gender and race, and "subconsensual" attributes that involve judgments about the self ("I am a good student"). Judgments about the self collectively constitute what has been called self-esteem or self-efficacy. Self-esteem thus describes the evaluative part of the self-concept and includes both positive and negative evaluations.

A concept that is closely related to that of self is identity. This term has become popular among writers and researchers interested in modern social movements, such as the feminist and gay rights movements, to describe identification with movement principles. In sociology, identity theory is largely associated with the work of S. Stryker and P. J. Burke: "Identity theory began by attempting to specify and make researchable the concepts of 'society' and 'self' in Mead's frame" (Stryker and Burke 2000, 285). For Stryker, identity is the empirically testable form of the self-concept.

Last year I attended a talk by historian Dan Diner, who argued that, in the case of ethnic identity, identity awareness arises from freedom of choice. When people are oppressed, they may take their identity for granted and not view it as a source of pride. This argument suggests that identity has a political component. Similarly, K. A. Cerulo (1997) claims that, in sociology, the concept of identity has come to coincide with the concept of collective identity. Thus identity is being used in a more specific sense than self to refer to the individual counterpart of group agency and political action. She argues further that identity reflects a conscious sense of the group as an agent and therefore becomes linked with an activist stance. M. Bernstein (2005) describes identity politics as a process through which identities are deployed strategically to bring about social change.

In this book, I use the term *identity* a little more broadly than those who argue for a political definition. *Disability pride* represents an ideal-typical identity that has come to be associated with disability rights activists; its polar opposite is *disability shame,* a view based on stigma. I would argue that individuals who are ashamed of their disabilities also have an identity, albeit an apolitical one. Shame, like pride, is learned in the course of interactions in groups and is a social construction. Thus, *disability identity* is used in this book to refer to that part of the self-concept that emerges from the disability-related self definitions that exist within an individual.

Two complementary versions of a theory of identity have developed: identity theory and social identity theory. M. A. Hogg and colleagues (1995, 255) explain that identity theory "is a microsociological theory that sets out to explain individuals' role-related behaviors," whereas social identity theory "is a social psychological theory that sets out to explain group processes and intergroup relations." As the authors note, identity theory's roots are in sociology, and social identity theory grew out of the discipline of psychology. J. E. Stets and P. J. Burke (2000) have argued that, although their terminologies differ, the theories have substantial similarities and can be linked. Because this book is primarily a work of sociology, I will use the terminology of identity theory to discuss the identities of individuals with disabilities.

G. J. McCall and J. L. Simmons (1978) describe the process of identification through which individuals categorize themselves as occupants of a role. Through interaction with other people, individuals learn about the social positions or statuses recognized in society and locate themselves within various categories, such as gender, race, or socioeconomic status: they learn that certain behaviors, or roles, tend to be associated with these statuses. Identities form through a process of identification with a variety of roles. Because they play multiple roles, individuals with disabilities have other identities in addition to their identity as a disabled person. In this book I focus on identity as a disabled person, or disability identity.

Because all individuals occupy a number of statuses and have the ability to play multiple roles, they must decide which role to play. In order to determine how to act in any given situation, the individual must first define the situation (Thomas 1928). Doing so requires the ability to take the role of the other, as described earlier, in order to choose the most appropriate role to play. Identity theorists refer to this process as role-choice behavior (Stryker and Burke 2000).

Stryker and Burke (2000) explain that the term *identity* refers to each of the group-based selves that a person occupies as a result of his or her social relationships, and *identities* are defined as internalized role expectations. These identities, in turn, are organized in a hierarchy of salience. Behavioral choices depend on which identities are most salient. For example, a woman may see herself as both a mother and a business owner, but if her identity as a mother is more salient, she may choose to stay at home with her child rather than go to the office on a day when the child is ill. Salience tends to be situational, varying with the role opportunities that present themselves at any point in time.

Stryker and Burke (2000, 286) also discuss the concept of commitment, which "refers to the degree to which persons' relationships to others in their networks depend on possessing a particular identity and role." In other words, interactions in some social groups are more valued (and often more frequent) than interactions in others. Commitment to the role relationships in these groups produces more highly salient identities. A related concept, significant others (Sullivan 1947), refers to those people whose opinions are most important to an individual. Interactions with significant others result in definitions that are more likely to be incorporated into a person's self-concept. T. Shibutani (1961) uses the term *reference groups* to describe those groups that are most important in shaping their members' perspectives.

The nature of a social structure may be important in determining commitment. Stryker and Burke (2000) note that the density of ties within a social network may be significant. Other characteristics of a network also play a role. For example, J. W. Kinch (1968) and others have discussed the role of frequency, intensity, duration, and recency of interactions in determining effects on self-concept.

Stryker and Burke (2000) argue that, through their behavior, individuals seek to maintain their existing identities or identity standards. They call this process self-verification. However, when individuals find themselves in new situations, new relationships may become significant to them. A. Strauss (1962) uses the phrase *turning points* to describe the times in people's lives when they encounter new groups, leading to relationships that change their identities. For example, when a student enters college, he or she is likely to meet other students and professors with ideas that are different from those encountered earlier in life. The student's own ideas and identity may change if these new relationships become significant.

Self-concept and identity exist within a person's mind. They are internal and only become apparent when a person plays a role. Behavior, or role playing, is the external manifestation of identity and the means by which others become aware of a person's identities and self-concept. Goffman (1958) contrasts "backstage" behavior, which is more or less automatic, with "front-stage" behavior that is intended to convey to others an actor's desired self. At job interviews, for example, people usually present themselves as capable of doing the job, whether or not they really believe in that capability. The others in the situation, in turn, make judgments about people based on their presented selves. Although role playing may or may not reflect a person's true identity, it is the basis on which people are typically judged.

The concept of identity, then, represents only one aspect of an individual's location in society. A broader concept that is useful in understanding the social location of individuals with disabilities is disability orientation, which has three related components: identity, model, and role. In the following paragraphs I briefly explain each one.

Identity has been described above as the empirically verifiable aspect of the self-concept that arises through social interaction. In the case of individuals with disabilities, two major disability-related identities have received attention in the literature: shame and pride. Shame presumably develops in response to interaction in a stigmatizing society. As noted earlier, disability pride has been identified in disability rights activists who reject society's devaluation of their disabilities. I have suggested elsewhere (Darling 2003) that both pride and shame are ideal types and that actual individuals may have elements of both in their identities.

Model refers to a paradigm or perspective related to a social condition such as disability. Those who subscribe to a medical model see disability as a form of illness and view people with disabilities as needing rehabilitation or cure. This model has been associated with the sick role (Parsons 1951), an undesirable state that requires the patient to cooperate with medical treatment in order to return to full participation in society. The sick role focuses on individual action rather than on social change. In this view, individuals with disabilities are commonly viewed as people to be pitied. The polar opposite of the medical model has been called the social model of disability (Oliver 1996). In this view, the locus of disability can be found in a society that fails to accommodate the diverse needs of individuals with disabilities. Those who subscribe to a social model see a need for social change in the form of physical changes to the environment, such as curb cuts and ramps, as well as changes in attitudes away from stigma and toward acceptance. Again, the medical and social models are ideal types that only approximate the views of actual individuals. As later chapters will show, most people adhere to some tenets of both models.

The third component of disability orientation is *role*, which encompasses the cluster of disability-related behaviors in which people with disabilities engage. Some may play the classic sick role and continue to search for cures for their impairments, whereas others may choose to forgo rehabilitative services. As I have explained elsewhere (Darling 2003), role choices are closely related to opportunities, which, in turn, are associated with one's location in society in terms of socioeconomic status (SES) and other statuses. Those who have been exposed only to the medical model may play the sick role because they are not aware of other behavioral options. Another role that has received considerable attention in the literature is disability rights activism. Activists join groups, participate in demonstrations, lobby their congressional representatives, or engage in other activities intended to increase opportunities for people with disabilities. The literature suggests that activists tend to espouse the social model of disability and to have disability pride; however, as I show later in this book, identity, model, and role are not always associated in expected ways. For example, some people with pride in their identities as individuals with disabilities reject activism and play a more passive role with respect to disability rights. The concept of disability orientation enables the exploration of other factors that may or may not be associated with disability identity.

Opportunity Structures

As noted earlier, identity, self, and disability orientation are believed to result from an individual's interactions in society in general and in smaller reference groups in particular. Microsociologists focus on these interactions and the selves and identities they engender. However, social structure plays an important role in determining where and whether interaction occurs. For example, individuals living in poverty with limited access to computers may not be aware of much of the culture of disability rights activism that can be found online. Thus, although role choice may involve a conscious decisionmaking process for those with access to multiple role options, it may not exist at all for others.

In this book, I use the concept of opportunity structure (Cloward and Ohlin 1960) to describe an individual's place in society with respect to opportunities for exposure to various identities and roles. Because of differences in SES, race and ethnicity, gender, age, area of residence, and other stratifying factors, not everyone is exposed equally to society's definitions and ideologies. Consequently, exposure to stigma or to the social model varies by opportunity structure. If symbolic interaction theory is correct, this diversity in exposure will result in a diversity of disability identities.

Disability and Impairment

Various terms have been used to describe conditions that deviate from social norms relating to appearance and functioning, most notably, *impairment, handicap,* and *disability.* The *International Classification of Functioning, Disability and Health,* 2nd ed., no longer includes the term *handicap* because of its pejorative connotations for some people (World Health Organization 1999). The document defines *impairments* as problems in body function or structure. Many would include mental function in this category as well. However, not all impairments limit or restrict participation in life activities; that is, they are not necessarily disabilities.

While recognizing the diversity of definitions that exist, in this book I adopt the terminology of the *International Classification of Functioning, Disability and Health* and most writers in the field of disability studies and use the term *impairment* to refer to an anatomical or physiological trait or condition. I use the term *disability* as it is defined in the Americans with Disabilities Act (ADA): "A physical or mental impairment that substantially limits one or more of the major life activities of such individual; a record of such an impairment; being regarded as having such an impairment" (Jones 2006, 4). Of particular importance in a sociological analysis such as the one in this book is the inclusion of the third element of the definition, "being regarded as having such an impairment." Although the bio-psychological consequences of an impairment may be significant for the person who has it and may contribute to the salience of the impairment in the person's mind, identity theory posits that only the definitions of other people are relevant in determining disability identity. In the perspective adopted here, disability is a social status, not a biological condition, and identification (or lack of identification) with the status is assumed to occur through social interaction.

2

Stigma and Acceptance over Time

As explained in the Introduction, people's identities have their genesis in the societies in which they live. Individuals' views of themselves are learned from the people with whom they interact. To understand disability identity, then, one needs to become familiar with societal views of disability and how they have changed over time. These views have varied both across cultures and within multicultural societies.

Cross-Cultural Views

As N. Groce (2005, 6) has written, "In all societies, individuals with disabilities are not only recognized as distinct from the general population, but value and meaning also are attached to their condition." Values attached to disability have varied both geographically and historically. Among the Songye of Zaire, a deformed child may be thrown into a river or buried in an anthill (Devlieger 2010), yet in some societies people with disabilities are believed to have supernatural powers and are held in high esteem. C. Safilios-Rothschild (1970) suggests that prejudice toward people with disabilities varies by (1) level of development and rate of unemployment; (2) beliefs about the role of government in alleviating social problems; (3) beliefs about individual "responsibility" (sin) for disability; (4) cultural values attached to different physical conditions; (5) disability-connected factors, including visibility, contagiousness, part of the body affected, physical versus mental nature of the disability, and severity of functional impairment; (6) effectiveness of public relations efforts; and (7) importance of activities that carry a high risk of disability—for example, war.

A sampling of variant reactions to disability in different cultures throughout the world illustrates the role of cultural values in shaping attitudes. Obesity in women has been greatly admired in most African tribes yet stigmatized in the American middle class (Chesler 1965). Among Middle Eastern Muslims, the term *saint* has been applied to people with an intellectual disability, and they have been given benevolent and protective treatment (Edgerton 1993). Similarly, B. A. Wright (1983) has noted that among the Wogeo, a New Guinea tribe, children with obvious deformities are buried alive at birth, but children disabled in later life are looked after with loving care. She notes that in some cultures some impairments, such as having extra fingers or toes, are considered lucky. Yet, among the Punan Bah of Borneo, people with severe deformities are classified as non-human and may not even be named (Nicolaisen 1995).

P. J. Devlieger (2010) states that in most African languages no term for disability exists. In Western languages, political and historical forces have led to the construction of disability as a cross-impairment concept derived from the common experiences of people with different disabilities. In Africa, however, this construction is not well developed, and languages only have words for specific impairments, such as blindness or lameness.

Using Nicaragua in the 1980s as his context, F. J. Bruun (1995, 200) has shown how politics can shape views of disability. Armed conflict during this period left many soldiers with disabilities. The government promoted the view that these soldiers were war heroes who should be held in high esteem, resulting in identity transformation: "[The soldier] came home mutilated. . . . His old identity was reduced by his inability to fulfill all his former roles. But as a soldier wounded in battle he got a new identity as a hero, an identity consciously created by the authorities." This finding supports the argument of Safilios-Rothschild described above that views of disability change according to social conditions.

Historical Context

J. Newman (1991) has suggested that attitudes and social policies with respect to persons with disabilities have resulted from historical processes guided by the philosophies of utilitarianism, humanitarianism, and human rights. These philosophies have been a part of Western culture for a long time and continue to shape attitudes and policy today.

M. Lazerson (1975) writes that the nineteenth century saw a shift in American society from home care of the child with a disability to institutionalization. He attributes this shift to the fears early and mid-nineteenth-century Americans had about social disorder. The creation of institutions paralleled the influx of large numbers of immigrants into the United States. As families became more transient, institutions outside the family began to assume certain welfare functions. Concurrently, any deviance from social norms, including disability, came to be defined as a social problem, not merely a family problem.

Safilios-Rothschild (1970) suggests that people with disabilities are a minority group in US society and share the following characteristics with other minority groups:

1. They are relegated to a separate place in society (encouraged to interact with their "own kind").
2. They are considered by the majority to be inferior.
3. Their segregation is rationalized as being "better for them."
4. They are evaluated on the basis of their categorical membership rather than their individual characteristics.

However, segregation of people with disabilities has been decreasing, and newer legislation, such as the Individuals with Disabilities Education Act (IDEA), has mandated integration and inclusion.

Lazerson (1975) attributes the shift away from institutions that took place in the twentieth century to the special education movement, which places the responsibility for educating children with disabilities onto community schools. In addition, inhumane conditions were found to exist in some large institutions. The success of some early efforts to provide family-based services to children led to the creation of more such programs. The success of community-based early intervention programs, in particular, began to be reported widely in the literature in the 1960s, resulting in the large-scale growth of these programs throughout the country. The availability of community resources, coupled with the spread of the ideology of normalization (Wolfensberger 1972), has once again made the family the locus of care for children with disabilities in the United States today. Institutional care of adults with disabilities also has declined over time, with the growth of group homes and other community-based facilities for people who are unable to live independently. However, institutions, and the ideologies on which they were based, continue to exist on a smaller scale in modern American society.

Deinstitutionalization, coupled with technological change and the removal of many barriers in the built environment, has increased the visibility of disability in modern society. When many people with disabilities were hidden at home or in institutions, public attitudes were often based on a fear of the unknown. However, as the following sections will show, greater visibility has not necessarily resulted in greater acceptance.

Modern Western Society

Stigma

The most pervasive attitude toward disability in modern Western society has been stigma. As Goffman (1963) and others have written, individuals with disabilities have commonly been discredited and relegated to a morally inferior status. Stigmatization is a form of societal reaction to those who are viewed as different because they do not conform to society's norms regarding appearance or behavior. H. Hahn (1988) describes the "aesthetic anxiety" that arises from interactions with individuals whose appearance does not conform to societal norms of physical attractiveness and the "existential anxiety," or threat of loss of functional capacities, experienced by people who interact with those who do not conform with society's norms relating to individual autonomy.

According to Goffman, stigma refers to a special kind of discrepancy between actual and virtual social identity and may take the form of slights, snubs, tactless remarks, or other forms of rejection: "While the stranger is present before us, evidence can arise of his possessing an attribute that makes him different from others in the category of persons available for him to be, and of a less desirable kind. . . . He is thus reduced in our minds from a whole and usual person to a tainted, discounted one" (Goffman 1963, 2–3).

Goffman applies the concept of stigma to groups as diverse as those with facial anomalies, crutch and wheelchair users, and those with blindness or deafness, as well as to people without disabilities whose appearance or behavior violates the social expectations of the majority, such as prostitutes and racial minorities. Stigma is, thus, culturally relative and is related to the values of the dominant group in a society. In American society, physical attractiveness, intelligence, and physical prowess tend to be highly valued, resulting in the stigmatization of those who deviate significantly from these ideals. Some studies have suggested that people with disabilities who also have other devalued statuses, such as women, racial minorities, and the poor, are likely to experience more complex stigma effects than those whose only difference is their disability. I discuss the interplay of multiple stigmatized statuses further in Chapter 4.

Although some studies have always repudiated the pervasiveness of stigma as a prime determinant of identity, most have accepted the basic tenets of Goffman's work and have tried to further his explanations about the effects of stigma. He was especially interested in interactions between stigmatized and nonstigmatized individuals. Stigma is most problematic in interactions with strangers because they are not aware of a person's true identity. Friends and family, however, are typically able to overlook an attribute that is discredited by others in society. Goffman cites two groups in which interactions are generally free of stigma: the "own" and the "wise." The own consists of others who also possess the discredited attribute, and the wise includes family members, professionals who work with persons with disabilities, and others who have frequent contact with such individuals. Sometimes, because of their association with those who are stigmatized, the wise come to acquire a "courtesy stigma" of their own.

Goffman suggests that potentially stigmatizing attributes may be either discredited or discreditable, depending on their visibility and obtrusiveness. He argues that, because of the negative consequences of stigmatization, people with discreditable attributes may try to pass as "normal," or to cover their attributes in order to make them less obtrusive. Passing and covering involve a process of information control. In passing, the individual attempts to prevent others from becoming aware of a potentially stigmatizing attribute. For example, a person who stutters when pronouncing certain sounds may avoid those sounds in conversation with strangers. Covering, on the other hand, applies to attributes that are discredited rather than discreditable. Covering involves attempts to minimize the obtrusiveness of a visible attribute. For example, a person with blindness may wear dark glasses to cover anomalies in the appearance of the eyes. C. Thomas (1999a, 54) quotes a woman without a hand: "I found the

SPRING CREEK CAMPUS

easiest solution was to hide my 'hand' in a pocket, and I became very skilled at this concealment. Thereafter, I always had to have clothes with a strategically placed pocket."

Such techniques of information control can reduce the interactional consequences of stigma awareness. A number of studies have shown that interactions between stigmatized and nonstigmatized individuals differ from those in which none of the interactants possesses a stigma. In the case of individuals with obvious disabilities, one study (Davis 1961) has suggested that interactions with "normals" proceed through three stages. At first, the nonstigmatized engage in "fictional acceptance" of persons with disabilities, pretending not to notice their stigmatizing features. For example, "normals" may avoid using words like *see* with someone who is blind. Most of the time, "normals" are unable to move beyond this stage and do not get to know people with disabilities very well. Sometimes, though, this stage is followed by "breaking through," in which a normalized projection of self of the person with a disability emerges. Finally, after a time, the stigmatized individual's moral normality may become institutionalized with only situational qualifications. This sequence of stages is more the exception than the rule, and typically "normals" never accept people with disabilities in more than a fictionalized manner. These interaction patterns have been confirmed in a number of experimental studies.

Although newer research in this area is lacking, anecdotal accounts continue to suggest the same kinds of interactional difficulties described in the earlier literature. E. Schecter (2012: 118, 121) describes her experience at a cocktail party she attended while wearing a leg brace and using metal crutches:

> I inch my way down the hall into the well-lit room, only to find myself at a wall of backs. Several people at the far side of this impenetrable circle catch a glimpse of my face, begin to smile, then notice my crutches. An iron mask on each face slams shut. . . . Before I was visibly disabled, I'd never gone to get-togethers where nobody but the hostess spoke to me. It happens all the time now in rooms full of strangers, even though I'm just as interested in meeting new people and hearing their stories as I've ever been.

The association of stigma with other variables. In addition to studies that have explored interaction patterns involving stigmatized individuals, a significant number of research studies have explored the relationship between stigma and a variety of other variables. One popular research theme has been the association between stigma and different impairments. Various empirical studies have confirmed the existence of stigma in the case of mental illness, Alzheimer's disease, major and minor bodily differences, wheelchair use, HIV/AIDS, epilepsy, deafness, mental retardation, autism, and other forms of physical disability (see, e.g., Becker 1980; Link et al. 1997; Schneider and Conrad 1980).

Variations in appearance, behavior, and degree of disability also seem to be associated with the presence and degree of stigma. A. J. Towler and D. J. Schneider (2005) have found that people tend to group stigmatizing conditions in separate categories, including physical disability, mental disability, economic disadvantage, social deviance, physical appearance, sexual identity, and racial identity. One study (Albrecht et al. 1982) has indicated that rejection is related primarily to disruption in social interaction. This finding was confirmed by a study (Baxter 1986) showing that the attribute most likely to attract attention to a child with a disability is speech, not appearance or behavior. As a result, families of children with speech differences tend to structure their lives to avoid situations that might require their child to speak, such as taking the child to see Santa Claus at Christmastime. Another study (Elliott et al. 1982) has suggested that the disruptive impact of stigma depends on the dimensions of visibility, pervasiveness, clarity, centrality, relevance, salience, responsibility for acquisition, and removability. In addition, many studies have suggested variations in stigmatization in different cultures and among subcultural groups within a society. Other studies (e.g., Link et al. 1997) have shown that even in the case of temporary disability, such as having a history of mental illness, stigma may persist long after the disability is gone.

Some studies have explored the occurrence of courtesy stigma in the cases of various disabilities and of people in a variety of relationships to stigmatized individuals. In particular, the existence of courtesy stigma has been especially well documented in the case of parents of children with autism, intellectual disability, and other impairments. Caregivers of people with Alzheimer's disease have also reported experiencing stigma in some social situations (Darling 2000b).

Studies of stigma management. Another major research theme has involved issues of stigma management, including the management of courtesy stigma. Some commonly used management techniques include concealing, reasoning, isolation, aggression, assertiveness, humor, withdrawal, negotiation, education, information control, and confrontation (see, e.g., Low 1996). These techniques are used by both individuals with disabilities and by their caregivers or associates. In the case of young children with developmental disabilities, for example, parents commonly lie about their children's ages to avoid stigma-provoking confrontations. As one mother said, "I never knew whether to give his right age, because other people got embarrassed. If it was just someone in a store, I just told them how old he *looked*" (Darling 1979, 157). A. Birenbaum (1970) notes the case of parents of children with intellectual disabilities who clean the house before visitors arrive to remove evidence of their children's destructive behavior. J. W. Schneider and P. Conrad (1980) report that such strategies can be learned from "coaches" and that they vary according to the social situation. In support groups and self-help groups, stigma management techniques are commonly a major discussion topic.

R. B. Edgerton (1993) conducted a long-term study of stigma management. He found that deinstitutionalized adults with mild intellectual disabilities engaged in a variety of passing and denial strategies, including concealing their institutional history, their sterilization scars, and their inability to read or do math. Many were able to succeed with the assistance of "benefactors," individuals without disabilities who performed necessary tasks that the ex-patients were unable to perform on their own and who assisted with passing and denial. Edgerton referred to a "benevolent conspiracy" that is essential for this population to have a successful life in the community.

In earlier research, Edgerton had concluded that "for all these persons, an admission of mental retardation is unacceptable—totally and without exception" (Edgerton 1993, 183). However, after a follow-up study he wrote, "A decade later, it was clear that a sense of stigma and a felt need to pass as normal were no longer central concerns for most of these people" (Edgerton 1993, 199). Further follow-up studies confirmed that most of these individuals had learned to play normative social roles and that "in most respects, the quality of their lives and the strength of their self-esteem were the equal of those seen among the nonretarded" (208).

Moving beyond stigma. The conclusions of Edgerton's later studies are similar to those found in much of the more recent literature on stigma. In contrast to most earlier studies, recent research and writing seem to suggest that, in many cases, individuals with disabilities have moved beyond stigma to establish positive identities. (I expand on the relationship between stigma and identity in Chapter 3.) Stigma may be decreasing to some extent as a result of recent policy changes and awareness initiatives that have resulted in increased access to social participation by persons with disabilities. Research suggests that stigma is inversely related to experience with people with stigmatized attributes (see, e.g., Hayward 2009). Thus, as social participation increases, stereotypes and fictional acceptance may eventually be replaced by more normalized views of people with disabilities. A number of recent studies have in fact shown that, in the case of a variety of groups with potentially stigmatizing attributes, including people with HIV/AIDS, congenital limb deficiencies, and severe burns, reported stigma is less than expected (Darling 2000b).

In further support of this trend, a special issue of the *Journal of Social Issues* that appeared in 1988, titled "Moving Disability Beyond 'Stigma,'" contained a series of articles suggesting that earlier assumptions about the universal nature of stigma were unfounded. In their introductory article in the issue, M. Fine and A. Asch (1988a) argue that earlier views linking disability and stigma are outmoded. Instead, they suggest a minority group framework, in which disability is defined in sociocultural rather than in medical or biological terms. In this view, people with disabilities are regarded as proactive shapers of societal responses rather than powerless victims. The volume chronicles numerous efforts by persons with disabilities and their advocates to overturn stigma-based models and their consequences. These include a movement by parents of children with disabilities that has focused primarily on issues of educational access and a movement by adults with disabilities that has worked to increase access in all areas of social life.

Much of the recent repudiation of stigma as the primary determinant of disability identity has been based in the disability rights movement. Although most literature that takes the effect of this movement into account dates from the late 1980s, as early as 1979 R. R. Anspach described the "identity politics" associated with political activism among people with disabilities. The disability rights movement, which played a major role in the passage of the Americans with Disabilities Act, locates the source of disability in an inequitable social structure rather than in the impairments of individuals. Thus, people with disabilities are seen as no different from others with minority group status, such as African Americans and gays and lesbians. These groups, too, were portrayed in the past as passive victims of stigma. Thanks to the civil rights and gay rights movements, society has become more inclusive. Consequently, stigma management techniques such as passing are being replaced by statements of pride in once-stigmatized identities. In this respect, the disability rights movement has much in common with other civil rights movements.

Another strand in recent literature that challenges older, stigma-based models describes strategies for promoting alternative, positive definitions of individuals with disabilities. The chief proponent of this approach, Wolf Wolfensberger, has proposed the concept of "social role valorization" (1995). As the opposite of stigmatization, social role valorization attaches positive meanings to attributes of disability. Such attributions raise the status of persons with disabilities and may have the effect of reversing the usual pattern and causing persons without disabilities to want to emulate those with them.

Although models like the minority group view and social role valorization seem to be spreading along with an increase in disability acceptance, stigmatizing attitudes and behaviors continue to exist in society today. (I present some of the evidence for the continued existence of stigma later in this chapter.) Clearly, some activists and others have embraced the newer models; however, as Chapters 6 and 7 show, many people with disabilities still seem to view their status through a lens of social stigma. As a result of social change, attitudes toward disability appear to be more diverse than they were in the past, so that the minority group or social model exists *alongside* the older medical and tragedy models. In the next section, I explore the diversity in attitudes among various subgroups within the larger population.

Subcultural Variation

In a pluralistic society, various groups *within* the society may hold divergent views of disability. Although these subcultures share some aspects of the larger society's culture, they also have their own beliefs, values, attitudes and norms, which are learned through interaction among their members. Societies are stratified along a number of different dimensions that are not mutually exclusive. Probably the most important dimension is socioeconomic status. In addition to socioeconomic stratification, differences based on race and ethnicity also occur. Religious and regional variations exist as well. A growing literature suggests that disability is viewed differently by various subcultural groups within American society.

Socioeconomic Status

One of the major bases of stratification in society is socioeconomic status. Most people interact largely with others who have similar levels of income, education, and occupational status. Numerous studies have found socioeconomic diversity regarding attitudes toward a variety of issues. Virtually all the studies that have looked at the relationship between SES and attitudes toward disability were conducted prior to 1980.

Some of the most interesting findings in these older studies have related to attitudes toward intellectual disability, especially in the mild ranges. Although professionals and others from middle- and upper-class backgrounds may regard mild intellectual disability as a devastating condition, lower-class individuals may not even define it as a disability. In a classic study of institutionalized children, J. R. Mercer (1965) found that the children who were discharged generally came from low-status families. High-status families were more likely to concur with official definitions of intellectual disability and the need for institutionalization. The low-status families, who were not as achievement-oriented, were able to envision their children playing normal adult roles. K. J. Downey (1963) found, similarly, that more educated families tended to show less interest in their institutionalized children because the children were unable to conform to the family's career expectations.

Lower-class families may have higher tolerance for deviance in general than middle-class families. S. Guttmacher and J. Elinson (1971) have found, for example, that upper-class respondents are more likely than lower-class respondents to define a series of deviant behaviors as illness. Middle- and upper-class families tend to share the professional's perspective of mental illness, whereas the lower classes may see such behaviors as normal variants. Children with disabilities that result in nonnormative behaviors may be less accepted in middle- and upper-class families as a result. Another explanation might be that disabilities of all kinds are simply more common in lower-SES groups and that familiarity leads to acceptance. However, this class-based pattern does not seem to occur as clearly in the case of physical disability. T. E. Dow (1966) has found no correlation between social class and parental acceptance of children with physical disabilities and notes that parents of all classes tend to have optimistic attitudes. These favorable attitudes are maintained by depreciating the importance of physique.

Recent studies of the influence of social class on attitudes toward disability are virtually nonexistent. Surprisingly, an extensive literature search revealed just one recent article that directly addressed this question. In a study of high school boys, M. Plata and J. Trusty (2005) discovered that those from low SES backgrounds were more willing to accept peers with learning disabilities than their higher SES counterparts, a finding reminiscent of those in the early studies reported above. Most recent studies have used SES as a control variable, *assuming* that it would affect attitudes.

Race and Ethnicity

Studies suggest that attitudes toward disability vary somewhat according to ethnic background. For example, in an Australian study, M. T. Westbrook and colleagues (1993) found that among the various ethnic groups they studied, Australians of German descent expressed the greatest acceptance of people with disabilities, whereas those of Arab descent expressed the least. Studies of attitudes in the United States toward disability have focused mostly on African Americans, Latino/as, and Asian Americans, and studies of Latino/as have been especially frequent. Throughout this discussion, the reader should keep in mind that *intragroup* variability is often greater than differences between groups and that stereotyping should be avoided.

African Americans. Several studies have suggested two themes characterizing African American attitudes toward disability: (1) stigma and (2) the notion that "We take care of our own." K. O. Conner and colleagues (2010) have reported stigma associated with seeking treatment for mental health disabilities among older African Americans, and S. V. King (1998) has argued that disability-related stigma may be as prevalent within the African American community as within the European American community. She found, in a small, qualitative study, that African American women with disabilities experienced pity, exclusion, and special treatment within their church communities. Her respondents reported being shunned or overprotected, and some noted others' adherence to a medical model that suggested they were in need of a cure. One mentioned this reaction: "Oh, you've got a disability, so I'm going to go pray for you. . . . You . . . need to get healed" (King 1998, 43). Similarly, Devlieger and colleagues (2007) have noted the absence of a disability culture and the social model among young, urban, African American men. However, F. Z. Belgrave (1998) has cited several studies suggesting more acceptance and positive attitudes toward people with disabilities among African Americans than among European Americans.

A number of studies have found that some African Americans treat disability as a community matter and avoid the services of professionals. P. S. Terhune (2005) reports the existence of two orientations among African American women caring for an adult child with a disability: a "secular professional discourse" and a "spiritual kin" discourse. Those with the latter orientation tended to rely on informal supports rather than seeking services from formal disability organizations. Conner and colleagues (2010) also report a reluctance to seek professional help among older African Americans. C. V. R. Willie and R. S. Reddick (2003) have noted the value of group responsibility in African American culture. Mutual help patterns are usually strong, and both family members and "fictive kin" commonly take responsibility for assisting family members with disabilities. Similarly, Belgrave (1998) cites a study showing greater support from extended family members among disabled African Americans than among whites. She notes that these African Americans were also more satisfied with the support they received from kin than comparable European Americans.

As noted in the Terhune study above, African American attitudes are not homogeneous. Higher SES individuals may hold attitudes toward disability that do not differ significantly from those of middle- and upper-class European Americans. In a study of parental values, J. Scanzoni (1985) found that SES was a more important determinant than race and that African American parents had the same values as European American parents of the same social class. Attitudes toward disability may, similarly, vary by SES, even within racial groups.

Latino/a Americans. Latino/a Americans constitute the largest ethnic minority in the United States. B. Harry (1992a) suggests that, although considerable intragroup diversity exists, Latino/a Americans tend to share a common language (Spanish) and worldview based on Catholic ideology, familism, and values of personalism, respect, and status. She suggests, further, that a strong sense of family pride sometimes makes acceptance of a severe disability difficult in these groups. Mild disability, however, may not even be recognized by the family.

Other studies suggest that some Latino/a cultural characteristics may assist in adaptation to individuals with disabilities. One study (Mary 1990) found that, in comparison with African American and European American mothers, Hispanic mothers were more resigned and less angry about having a child with intellectual disability. Similarly, Santiago-Rivera et al. (2002) note a study showing that lower-SES Latino/as tend to have lower expectations for developmental milestones in children, which could promote acceptance of those with developmental disabilities. Another group characteristic that would facilitate adaptation in the case of children unable to achieve independence during adolescence and adulthood is continuing interdependence between parents and their adult children.

Although similarities exist among various groups of Latino/a origin, Mexicans, Puerto Ricans, and other Latino/a Americans have separate identities and subcultures. The literature on attitudes toward disability has focused on Mexican Americans and Puerto Rican Americans, groups with large numbers of lower-SES members.

The Mexican American population is the most youthful and rapidly growing ethnic minority in the United States (Martinez 1999). Mexican Americans tend to be geographically concentrated in the southwestern states, and many maintain strong ties to family in Mexico. However, recent immigrants may have different characteristics from those who are US-born (Baca Zinn and Pok 2002).

The importance of the extended family in Mexican culture has been noted by many writers. S. S. Santana-Martin and F. Santana (2005) suggest that in Mexican culture, the family is expected to care for members with disabilities. In an analysis of multiple studies of Mexican American attitudes toward disability, J. F. Smart and D. W. Smart (1991) cite a number of cultural values that tend to promote acceptance of disability, including familism, cohesiveness, protectiveness, and stoic attitudes toward life in general.

In a study of Mexicans and Mexican Americans living on the Texas-Mexico border, Graf and colleagues (2007) found pity for persons with disabilities, and many of their respondents agreed that such persons should stay at home. However, they held positive attitudes toward family members with disabilities and did not believe that it was embarrassing to have such a family member. Their general attitudes reflected kindness rather than stigma. These attitudes contrast with those of the general, non-Latino population discussed earlier.

Like other ethnic groups, Mexican Americans, depending on their degree of identification with the traditional culture, may have folk beliefs about the nature of disease and disability. Smart and Smart (1991) and Santana-Martin and Santana (2005) note, for example, that Mexicans may regard illness or disability as a punishment for sin or wrongdoing. Santana-Martin and Santana (2005) note that Mexican parents are more likely to blame themselves in the case of mental disability; physical disability, however, is viewed as "normal."

Although many Mexican American families may behave in the ways suggested above, many others exhibit attitudes and behavior that do not differ significantly from those of Anglo or other non-Mexican families. One study of poor Mexican mothers (Shapiro and Tittle 1986) found that like their Anglo counterparts, they experienced difficulties in the areas of social support, child adjustment, perceived stress, and family functioning as a result of their children's disabilities. Similarly, a study of amniocentesis decisions by Mexican-origin women (Browner, Preloran, and Cox 1999) found that health care providers incorrectly assumed that decisions would be governed by "deep-rooted, cultural givens," such as opposition to abortion. In fact, these women's decisions were related more to such variables as their understanding of risks and their faith in their doctors. Graf and colleagues (2007, 162) note with regard to their study of attitudes toward disability, "our results . . . confirm that . . . persons living in this border region are diverse in their beliefs and that, therefore, assignment of views about disability must be made cautiously."

Perhaps even more than other ethnic groups, the Puerto Rican community relies very heavily on the family as a source of strength and support. Another frequently noted aspect of the Puerto Rican subculture is fatalism (see, e.g., García-Preto 1982; Ghali 1977). Submissiveness and acceptance of fate are encouraged, in contrast with the American values of achievement and aggressiveness. As in the Mexican American subculture, such fatalism may help people cope with disabilities.

Harry (1992b) has noted that the low-income Puerto Rican families in her study did not accept professional definitions of their children's disabilities because of different meanings they attached to the terms *handicapped* or *retarded*. One parent said, "They say the word 'handicap' means a lot of things. . . . But for us, Puerto Ricans, we still understand this word as 'crazy'" (31). Similarly, M. E. Gannotti and colleagues (2001) found that Puerto Rican parents' attitudes toward child development and disability differed from US norms. In particular, these parents valued interdependence and *sobre protectiva* (overprotectiveness) and did not define their children's continuing dependence in negative terms.

As in the case of other ethnic groups, Puerto Rican values tend to change with increasing acculturation. H. Carrasquillo (2002) has noted that, although familism is still an important value among second-, third-, and fourth-generation Puerto Ricans, it is not as strong as among first-generation immigrants.

Asian Americans. Asian Americans are the third-largest ethnic minority group in the United States. The income levels of Asian Americans are high relative to those of other ethnic minorities, but those from Southeast Asia tend to be relatively disadvantaged (Paniagua 1998). Just as one should not necessarily generalize from one Latino group to another, one must be careful in assuming that all Asian subcultures are alike. Yet similarities do exist.

Like other ethnic groups, many Asian Americans value the family highly. Family problems are regarded as private, and bringing them to the attention of outsiders is considered shameful (Shon and Ja 1982). Harry (1992a) has written that the essence of Eastern cultures is collectivism and harmony, and that modesty is important. She notes that major disabilities are traditionally interpreted in one of four ways: (1) as retribution for sins of the parents or ancestors, (2) as possession by evil spirits, (3) as resulting from the mother's behavior during pregnancy, or (4) as an imbalance in physiological function. Such disorders are therefore seen as bringing shame to the family and may be met with fatalism or folk healing. However, like other ethnic groups, Japanese Americans are becoming increasingly acculturated to US patterns, and Takagi (cited in Ishii-Kuntz 1997, 145) states, "it is now difficult to speak of a singular Japanese American family experience."

Among Chinese Americans as well, the family—not the individual—is the major unit of society. Traditionally the Chinese tend to be fatalistic and to believe in collective responsibility among kin (Gould-Martin and Ngin 1981; Lee 1982). Chinese parents typically have high educational aspirations for their children (Harrison et al. 1984). Acceptance of a child with an intellectual disability could be problematic within such a value orientation, and Yee (1988) has, in fact, noted that denial of a child's disability is common in Asian families. Wang and colleagues (cited in Liu 2005) suggest that the Chinese are more positive toward people with physical disabilities than toward people with developmental or mental disabilities. G. Z. Liu (2005) notes, further, that Chinese people are generally more accepting of acquired than of congenital disability.

As in the case of other ethnic groups, however, considerable intragroup variability is likely to be present among Asian American families, especially those with long exposure to mainstream American culture. E. N. Glenn and S. G. H. Yap (2002) note, for example, that Chinese American professional families resemble other families of similar socioeconomic status regardless of ethnicity.

In summary, members of racial and ethnic minority groups may or may not hold the same attitudes toward disability as others in society. Although recent studies on social class are lacking, SES may be a more important indicator of attitudes than either race or ethnicity. Studies of lower-SES African Americans and Latino Americans suggest an absence of familiarity with or adherence to a social model of disability. Stigma toward people with disabilities appears to be stronger among African Americans and Asian Americans than among Latino Americans, but considerable intragroup variability appears to exist.

Cultural Representations of Disability in the Media

The media tend to reflect the attitudes toward disability that are present in society. Various studies have looked at the depiction of people with disabilities in literature, film, television, and advertising and have generally concluded that most images have been stereotypical, although realistic portrayals are becoming more common. R. S. Black and L. Pretes (2007), among others, have noted the following stereotypes: (1) pitiable and pathetic; (2) "supercrip"; (3) sinister, evil, and criminal; (4) better off dead; (5) maladjusted—own worst enemy; (6) burden to family and/or society, and (7) unable to live a successful life.

Pitiable and pathetic characters include Tiny Tim in *A Christmas Carol*. As J. Shapiro (1994) and others have noted, these characters are portrayed as helpless and in need of caring and a cure. F. Whittington-Walsh (2002) notes the association between being dependent and being asexual. She describes the absence of sexuality in many disabled characters. P. K. Longmore (2003) adds that these characters are also sometimes portrayed as sexually incapacitated.

The supercrip stereotype suggests that characters with disabilities need to compensate for their disabilities with extraordinary talents (Longmore 2003). Whittington-Walsh (2002) cites movies like *Rain Man*, with its autistic savant character, as examples of this genre. Others include depictions of outstanding feats accomplished by athletes with disabilities.

Many novels and films include a villain with a disability or deformity—Captain Hook, Long John Silver, or Dr. Strangelove. Longmore (2003, 133) writes, "Among the most persistent [melodramatic devices] is the association of disability with malevolence. Deformity of body symbolizes deformity of soul." He argues that giving disabilities to villainous characters reinforces common beliefs that disability is a punishment for evil, that disabled people are embittered, and that people with disabilities resent the nondisabled.

A number of films, such as *Whose Life Is It Anyway?*, have featured people with disabilities who want to die. Such stories assume that life with a disability is not worth living. Longmore (2003) argues that disability is equated with a loss of one's humanity in these films.

Disabled characters also are commonly depicted as maladjusted or isolated, unable to engage in normal social relationships. As the next chapter will show, the theme of psychological maladjustment was also common in much of the early academic literature on disability. Longmore (2003) and others have noted that this theme characterizes the medical or personal model of disability, in which the disabled individual is "blamed" for his or her inability to "adjust"—as opposed to the social model, in which isolation is attributed to society's lack of acceptance.

More recently, these stereotypes have been replaced in some cases by more normalized images of people with disabilities. Shapiro (1994), Longmore (2003), and others have noted that, interestingly, advertising has led the way in portraying people with disabilities as "ordinary." Commercials and print advertisements often show children and adults with disabilities using the products they are trying to sell, perhaps because they recognize that people with disabilities and their families constitute a potential market for their goods. However, alongside these newer images, stereotypical portrayals continue to exist.

Continuing Evidence of Stigma

Although attitudes toward disability appear to be changing to some extent, evidence of stigma can be found in many areas of life. People with disabilities continue to experience discrimination in employment, education, and social opportunities. For example, the employment-population ratio for people with disabilities in 2010 was 18.6, compared with a ratio of 63.5 for people without disabilities (US Bureau of Labor Statistics 2011). Although many people with disabilities are over age 65, persons with disabilities were much less likely to be employed than those without disabilities in every age group. People with disabilities are also more likely to be victims of abuse and hate crimes. In 2010, the age-adjusted violent victimization rate for persons with disabilities was almost twice the rate among persons without disabilities (US Bureau of Justice Statistics 2011). Women and children with disabilities are especially likely to experience abuse (Foster and Sandel 2010). Recent studies also show the persistence of negative attitudes toward persons with disabilities (see, e.g., Shannon et al. 2009). Thus, although their situation is improving to some extent, people with disabilities continue to experience stigma and unequal treatment in today's society.

Conclusion: Societal Views of Disability

To the extent that individuals with disabilities interact with the societies around them, they are likely to be exposed to the societal views of disability described in this chapter. These views continue to change as newer models and definitions become more widespread. During most of the twentieth century, the prevailing view of disability involved stigma, and the personal or medical model dominated expressions of popular culture. Some subcultural variability existed in these views, but most racial and ethnic groups seem to have adopted at least some tenets of the personal model, such as pity. More recently, views have included both elements of stigma and newer social model concepts, like the ordinariness of people with disabilities. Thus, people with disabilities may encounter a variety of definitions of themselves as they interact in society today.

3

Societal Views and Self-Conceptions

In Chapter 2, I suggested that societal views of disability have been predominantly negative. However, these views have changed somewhat over time. Today, elements of both the medical/personal model and the social model can be found in various segments of the population. In this chapter I explore the relationship between societal views and how people with disabilities view themselves. Symbolic interaction theory suggests that self-views reflect those of society. Thus, one might expect a trend toward more positive self-appraisals among people with disabilities in response to the social changes reported in Chapter 2. However, individual internationalization of macro-level social change depends on micro-level processes.

The Looking-Glass Self and the Labeling Perspective

The symbolic interaction perspective suggests that a person's self-concept derives from definitions he or she has received from interacting in society. The looking-glass self reflects the appraisals received from others. During the 1960s and early 1970s, the labeling perspective in sociology associated with H. S. Becker (1963), E. M. Lemert (1967), and others posited that stigmatized individuals would see themselves as others saw them and would have a deviant identity. Erving Goffman explains that a child with a stigmatized attribute will have a "moral experience" when first exposed to the evaluations of society, often upon school entrance, when the child is labeled as different: "[The child] will be told that he will have an easier time of it among 'his own,' and thus learns the own he thought he possessed was the wrong one, and that this lesser own is really his" (Goffman 1963, 33).

Labeling theorists argued that stigmatized individuals were expected to play a deviant role in society and would only be rewarded if they played the role that had been bestowed on them. Playing this role, in turn, reinforced a person's deviant identity. Thus, individuals who had been labeled as deviant entered into a pattern or "career" of deviance, in which they continued to conceive of themselves and to act according to the expectations of others. For example, a child with a disability might be rejected by a "normal" peer group and have no choice but to associate with a group of disabled peers. As a result, the child would learn to accept a stigmatized identity and would no longer try to play the role of a "normal" child. The labeling perspective dominated sociological thinking about disability until the 1980s, when other models began to gain ground. Other fields also assumed that individuals with disabilities would have negative self-views. Most of the studies that tried to measure self-concept directly prior to 1980 were done by psychologists and psychiatrists. Although these studies often used faulty methodology and have since been refuted by newer evidence, they are included in the section below for their historical interest—they clearly show the influence of negative societal views on the researchers of the time.

Early Studies of Self-Esteem in People with Disabilities

Unlike sociologists who believed that the roots of negative self-views in people with disabilities lay in society, psychoanalysts focused on the body. Psychoanalytic theory classically posited a strong relationship between people's feelings about their bodies and their level of psychological adjustment. As a result, psychiatrists and psychologists who used psychoanalysis tended to question the mental well-being of persons with bodily aberrations of various kinds. Many of the early studies used children, rather than adults, as subjects, perhaps because of the availability of large numbers of institutionalized children during the polio epidemics of the 1950s. E. P. Bernabeu (1958) argued that the young polio patients in her study used inappropriate and pathogenic defenses to handle feelings of frustration, anxiety, and rage, and in a study of children with physical disabilities, M. D. Schechter (1961) noted an "ever-present thinly disguised depression in all these children." These studies are typical of a number of early studies conducted with hospitalized samples. Certainly, children who are undergoing medical treatment and who are separated from their families might be expected to be anxious or depressed—regardless of whether or not they had disabilities.

Another type of study based on psychoanalytical principles used projective techniques to evaluate the self-esteem and emotional problems of children with disabilities. A popular technique in studies of this kind was the Draw-a-Person Test (DAP), in which subjects are asked to draw a person of each sex and then to draw themselves. The DAP, like other projective techniques, has been criticized for its questionable validity, reliability, and meaning (see, e.g., Wylie 1974). Using this technique, B. A. Wysocki and E. Whitney (1965) found, in a comparison of fifty disabled and fifty nondisabled children, that the children with disabilities showed greater feelings of inferiority, anxiety, and aggression ("evidenced" by factors such as figure size, pressure, and shading).

In other studies using the DAP, trained judges were unable to distinguish the drawings of children with disabilities from those of a nondisabled control group. In an analysis of the drawings of twenty-two individuals who had had polio, A. B. Silverstein and H. A. Robinson (1956) found that judges who knew in advance that their subjects had disabilities found evidence of these disabilities in their drawings. In a second stage of the study, a nondisabled, matched comparison group was added, and the judges were no longer able to tell the drawings of the two groups apart. Similarly, in a study of twenty-six children with upper-extremity amputation and a matched control group, judges were able to distinguish self-portraits of those with amputations from those without amputations but could not tell which subjects were disabled when the generic Draw-a-Person test was used. Further, the children with amputations did not show greater conflict or anxiety. The authors concluded that "the amputee children . . . in the main represent their bodies and those of others realistically and, on the whole, nondefensively" (Centers and Centers 1963, 165).

Thus, well-designed studies using the variable of body image did not demonstrate any clear feelings of inferiority among people with disabilities. The labeling theorists' contention that stigmatized individuals accept society's definition of them was, consequently, not supported. However, some support for labeling theory can be found in a few older studies that measured self-esteem in other ways. For example, J. H. Meyerowitz (1962) found that a group of children labeled as "educable mentally retarded" attending a regular school had more negative self-concepts than a group of typical children. Similarly, when presented with a series of pictures of children with and without disabilities, both the disabled and nondisabled children in one study (Richardson et al. 1961) chose the picture of the nondisabled child as the one they liked best.

In another study (Richardson et al. 1964), children with slight-to-moderate physical disabilities were asked to talk about themselves. These children made a slightly larger proportion of negative statements than a nondisabled group (13 percent vs. 8 percent for boys; 17 percent vs. 11 percent for girls). Of course, these percentages indicate that from 83 percent to 87 percent of the statements made by the children with disabilities were positive, suggesting that negative views did not predominate in this sample.

Some other early studies that measured self-concept directly did not support the contention that stigmatized individuals accept society's negative definition. For example, in a comparison of twenty-nine children with congenital blindness with an equal number of sighted children, M. Zunich and B. E. Ledwith (1965) found little difference in self-esteem between the two groups. Similarly, C. L. Mayer (1967) found that children with intellectual disabilities did not necessarily have low self-esteem.

Other studies looked at variables such as gender and degree of disability in relation to self-esteem. S. J. Smits (1964) found, for example, that adolescents with severe disabilities had significantly lower self-esteem scores than adolescents with mild disabilities. In addition, women with severe disabilities had significantly lower scores than severely disabled men. Another study (Meissner et al. 1967), using a sample of high school juniors, found no correlation between obviousness or impact of disability and self-concept. When gender was held constant, however, women with the highest-impact and most obvious disabilities had low self-esteem, whereas men with similar disabilities had high self-esteem. Thus, gender differences may play some role in self-concept formation. I discuss this finding further in Chapter 4.

In summary, some poorly designed early studies seemed to indicate that individuals with disabilities had low self-esteem and consequent maladjustment. These studies seemed to reflect the biases of researchers exposed to the societal stigma that was pervasive at the time. However, other studies had mixed results, and little evidence existed to support the contention of labeling theorists that societal stigma would be internalized and reflected in the self-concepts of people with disabilities.

Recent Studies

According to S. Sze and S. Valentin (2007), recent studies show that children with disabilities do not necessarily have poor self-images, and most studies of children and young adults in the 2000s have found little difference in self-esteem between those with and those without disabilities. For example, T. R. Blake and J. O. Rust (2002) recorded similar self-esteem and self-efficacy scores in samples of college students with and without disabilities. Similarly, in a study of self-esteem and empathy in preadolescents, N. Griffin-Shirley and S. L. Nes (2005) found no difference between sighted and visually impaired participants. In a Dutch study of children with cerebral palsy, Schuengel and colleagues (2006) reported that self-worth and perceived competence were comparable to those recorded in a normative sample, and an Australian study of children with intellectual disabilities (Huck et al. 2010) found that perceived self-competence was positive and comparable to that reported for other populations with and without disability. Although they did not use a comparison group, S. Glenn and C. Cunningham (2001) found, using several measures of self-esteem, that young adults with Down syndrome rated themselves positively on all measures. Finally, a Swedish study of children and adolescents with mobility impairments (Jemta et al. 2009) discovered relatively high levels of both dimension-specific and global self-esteem.

A few studies have looked at domain-specific measures of self-esteem. For example, D. R. Shapiro and J. J. Martin (2010) studied aspects of "physical self-concept" in a sample of athletes with physical disabilities. Their respondents reported mostly positive perceptions of self-esteem, global physical self-concept, endurance, body fat, sports competence, strength, flexibility, and physical activity. S. Cragg and K. Lafreniere (2010) compared self-esteem and body image in a sample of women with Turner syndrome (associated with short stature and other physical characteristics) and in a typical group of female college students. Although scores on performance-related self-esteem did not differ between the two groups, the women with Turner syndrome scored significantly lower on "body esteem" and on general, social, and appearance-related self-esteem.

Having low "body esteem" would not necessarily result in low overall self-esteem if the importance of physical appearance were discounted. Shapiro and colleagues (2008) looked at global self-worth, along with domain-specific ratings of importance in a sample of children with visual impairments. They found that the children discounted the importance of physical appearance, athletic competence, and social acceptance and had moderately high global, or overall, self-esteem. Thus, along with the appraisals of themselves that people receive in the course of interaction in society, they also learn that some traits are more important than others. Consequently, a person with appearance traits that deviate from the norm may still have high self-esteem if appearance is deemed less important than other traits, such as character or personality. One older study (Dow 1966) found that parents of children with disabilities depreciated the importance of physique and were thus able to maintain optimistic attitudes toward their children's disabilities. Children raised with such attitudes are likely to internalize them and use them in their self-appraisals.

Although, overall, self-esteem appears to be equally high in disabled and nondisabled samples, a few studies have found negative self-perceptions, notably among women with disabilities. In an Israeli study, I. Duvdevany (2010) found that self-esteem and perceived quality of life scores of women with physical disabilities were significantly lower than those of a comparison group. The women with disabilities were also less likely to be married, had less education, and were less likely to be employed. The differences were more significant among younger adult women than among older women. Similarly, in a US study, M. A. Nosek et al. (2003) found that women with disabilities had significantly lower self-esteem and self-cognition (perceptions of how others saw them) than women without disabilities. The disabled women also had greater social isolation, less education, and lower rates of employment. Finally, V. Moin and colleagues (2009) found that women with disabilities had significantly lower body image, sexual self-esteem, sexual satisfaction, and life satisfaction scores than a nondisabled comparison group. (For more on the relationships among gender, disability, and self-concept, see Chapter 4.)

Contrary to the findings of other research on children with disabilities, F. Soyupek and colleagues (2010) found that the children with cerebral palsy in their sample had self-concepts that were significantly less favorable than those of a control group. However, the study was conducted in Turkey, and the findings may reflect attitudes in that particular culture that differ from those in other Western societies.

Several studies have looked at other variables in relation to self-esteem. For example, in a study of persons with psychiatric disabilities, K. K. Sang and C. T. Mowbray (2005) found that household income, diagnosis, perceived stigma, and other factors were related to self-esteem. Degree of disability may also be important. In a meta-analysis of studies of self-esteem in young people with physical disabilities, M. Miyahara and J. Piek (2006) concluded that minor disabilities had a moderate effect on self-esteem, whereas major disabilities had only a mild effect. Perhaps people with severe disabilities are more isolated from mainstream society and less subject to the effects of normative definitions. Social support also appears to make a difference. In a study of children, teens, and young adults with physical disabilities, B. J. Antie (2004) determined that perceived social support from parents was the strongest predictor of global self-worth.

Another variable that seems to affect self-esteem is the timing of disability acquisition. L. Jemta and colleagues (2009) found that among the children and adolescents they studied, those with acquired impairments had lower global self-esteem than those whose impairments were congenital. They report that those with acquired impairments express regrets about the loss of their identity. This finding has also been reported elsewhere, and I discuss it further in Chapter 8.

Overall, then, the literature suggests that the self-esteem of people with disabilities is not very different from that of the population as a whole. Although some people with disabilities, notably some women, those with acquired disabilities, and those with milder disabilities, do appear to have internalized society's negative appraisals, most seem to be able to maintain positive self-views in a stigmatizing society. In the next section, I explore this apparent lack of support for looking-glass self theory.

Reference Groups and Significant Others

B. Major and L. T. O'Brien (2005, 394) write, "Importantly, stigma is relationship- and context-specific; it does not reside in the person but in a social context." In the case of another group that has experienced stigma, African Americans, psychologists and sociologists argued for a long time that the group's minority racial status would produce low self-esteem in comparison with European Americans. However, actual studies showed that, in fact, the self-esteem of African Americans did not differ significantly from that of the majority, and at least one study (cited in Major and O'Brien 2005) found that African Americans had higher self-esteem than European Americans. One older study that attempted to explain this apparent paradox (Rosenberg and Simmons 1971) noted that African American children in predominantly African American schools had higher self-esteem than those in schools in which they were in the minority. They argued that children interact largely in primary groups of others like themselves and that these groups serve to insulate them from society's negative definitions and to protect their self-esteem. In other words, their reference groups may be different from those of the majority group.

People tend to pay attention to definitions from others who are important to them, that is, their significant others (Sullivan 1947). Typically, significant others include family members and close friends, as well as experts of various kinds, such as physicians or members of the clergy. Not surprisingly, numerous studies have indicated strong correlations between the opinions of children and those of their parents. The concept of reference group (Shibutani 1955) is closely related to that of significant others, but derives from a sociological rather than a psychological tradition. Reference groups are those from which people derive their perspectives. T. Shibutani (1955, 564) writes, "Through direct or vicarious participation in a group one comes to perceive the world from its standpoint." High school students, for example, are likely to evaluate their grades in terms of the grades their friends receive. Thus, students with a C average might not be upset if most of their friends had similar averages. However, students with a C average whose friends all received As might feel a need to improve.

Shibutani points out that people typically internalize their perspectives through direct interaction with their significant others. However, he notes that sometimes social participation is vicarious and norms and expectations may be internalized through exposure to books or other media. Certainly in today's world of electronic communication, people are easily exposed to ideas and definitions they may not have encountered in their everyday, face-to-face interactions with family and friends.

Who, then, are the reference groups of people with disabilities? For most people, reference groups and significant others change to some extent over the life course. All the child development literature suggests that during childhood, and often later as well, parents are the most important significant others. The importance of parents as the primary socializing agents for their children makes sense theoretically and has been demonstrated empirically in numerous studies. High parent-child correlations have been found on attitudes ranging from religion and politics to self and role.

Because children with disabilities are perhaps even more likely than other children to depend on their parents, their views are especially likely to be shaped by parents and close family members during the childhood years. One might expect, then, that children whose parents accepted their children's disabilities would have higher self-esteem than those whose parents did not. In support of this expectation, S. Coppersmith (1967) found a correlation between children's self-esteem and their mothers' reasons for having children. Mothers who viewed having children as a "natural event" tended to have children with higher self-esteem, whereas those who wanted children for personal reasons had children with lower self-esteem. Children who are unable to live up to their parents' expectations are less likely to think highly of themselves. Children with disabilities might be less likely than other children to be the "ideal" children their parents envisioned, perhaps resulting in lower self-esteem. The fact that most children with disabilities do not have low self-esteem suggests that most parents accept their children, regardless of their disabilities. In the case of children with intellectual disabilities, S. Beart and colleagues (2005) cite several studies showing that parents sometimes try to protect their children by preventing their exposure to negative definitions.

However, some parents may reinforce society's negative attitudes, as this account (Danielson 2004, 9) illustrates: "Unfortunately, I . . . learned from my family that my disability, while not a problem at home, was not acceptable in public—as if my [disability] were a shameful secret. My parents never actually said that to me, but I believed JRA [juvenile rheumatoid arthritis] was not acceptable because it was never mentioned at home." L. Blumberg (2004, 24) points out that parents and children may have very different views of disability: "For parents, disability may be an unplanned surprise . . . a tragedy, touching and poignant. For the child, it may just be a given, something that is natural."

In particular, children with disabilities are unlikely to be exposed to an identity of "affirmation" during childhood. As one disabled adult said, "You cannot have a pride or rights-asserting identity if you do not know that such identities even exist in the world" (quoted in Seligman and Darling 2007, 175). Moreover, many children with disabilities have little exposure to adults with disabilities; as a result, their role models may be the nondisabled "heroes" admired by children in general—media celebrities or star athletes. When these figures serve as reference groups for disabled children, the children's self-esteem might be negatively affected because they cannot envision themselves emulating their heroes. Sometimes, though, early exposure to a disabled adult may have a positive impact: "I remember at wheelchair training when I was little, we had an instructor who used a chair and that was my first contact with someone who well, was an adult and that was really important to see that he has a chair and sits there and that it works out okay" (Barron 1997, 235).

Reference groups tend to change as children grow and spend more time away from home. A. Strauss (1962) introduced the concept of *turning points* to describe situations during which individuals are exposed to new significant others. Common turning points include college entrance, starting a new job, getting married, and moving to a new community. These "status passages" involve learning new roles and, often, acquiring new identities as a result. For example, a common impetus to religious conversion is falling in love with someone of a different religion from one's own.

In the past, children with significant disabilities commonly continued to live with their parents well into adulthood, in part because appropriate alternative living arrangements were not available. As society has become more accessible and community living options have increased, people with disabilities have had more opportunities to interact with a wider range of people. In addition, widespread use of the Internet has allowed people with disabilities to "meet" others both like and unlike themselves, increasing their exposure to both stigma and acceptance by people outside their immediate families.

Other Variables in Self-Concept Formation

Certainly, the source of definitions of the self is an important variable in determining whether definitions are internalized. As I suggested in the previous section, definitions from significant others and reference groups are more likely than definitions from unimportant others to be incorporated into a person's self-concept, and the closer the relationship to the evaluator, the more likely the evaluation will be accepted. However, the significance of the other is not the only variable that matters. In addition, the nature, frequency, intensity, and recency of a definition play a role, along with the characteristics of the issuer and recipient of the definition and those of the situation or context.

J. W. Kinch (1968) hypothesized that four factors influenced whether or not definitions received from others were incorporated into a person's self-concept: frequency of the definition, perceived importance of the other, temporal proximity, and consistency. A series of experimental studies supported the link between frequency and internalization but showed that *in*consistency in definitions received resulted in greater self-concept change than consistency. This finding suggests that the direction of a definition might be important. For example, people who have heard many negative definitions of themselves might be swayed by a single, positive definition.

The importance of direction has been confirmed in other studies. In an analysis of studies of social feedback and self-appraisals, D. C. Lundgren (2004) found that research supports the association between resistance to negative evaluations and acceptance of positive evaluations. Lundgren reported that the stronger the negative affect associated with an evaluation, the greater the tendency to reject the evaluation. Thus, individuals with disabilities might be more likely to be influenced by even a few positive definitions of themselves, even though they are also exposed to the negative feedback of a stigmatizing society.

Preexisting beliefs also seem to play a role in whether or not an individual internalizes stigmatizing appraisals of the self. People who acquire disabilities later in life may remember negative, often stereotypical, images of people with disabilities from their childhood. E. Schecter (2012, 109–110) describes her thoughts as a young adult upon receiving her crutches for the first time:

> Flash! I'm six years old, staring with reverence, revulsion, and terror at one of the Easter Seals Posters that pop up like crocuses every spring. This year, a darling little girl smiles bravely back at me. . . . Her radiant smile lights up her perfect skin, perfect teeth, perfect eyes—everything's perfect except the wretched braces of metal and leather buckled like cages around her legs, and the hideous crutches with metal arm-bands that circle her dimpled elbows. . . . She's the child I never want to be: a child who thinks

she's beautiful but is, in my eyes, just an ugly polio-child begging for dimes.

In contrast, Major and O'Brien (2005) note that those who believe that discrimination against the stigmatized is unjust are less likely to incorporate societal stigma into their self-concepts and that those who identify strongly with the stigmatized community may also be immune to the negative effects of stigma on the self; however, they cite one study showing that some members of stigmatized groups may decrease their involvement in those groups as a protection against stigma. They note the variability in self-esteem within stigmatized groups and even within the same individual in different contexts.

The nature of an impairment may affect the internalization of stigma as well. Those with significant cognitive impairments may not have the role-taking skills to understand and internalize negative definitions they receive from others (Beart et al. 2005). However, as Beart and colleagues (2005), R. B. Edgerton (1993), and M. Rapley and colleagues (1998) have shown, many individuals with intellectual disabilities are aware of the stigma attached to their disabilities and develop strategies for seeing themselves in positive ways.

Self-Concept and Disability Identity

As noted in Chapter 1, identity is one aspect of the self-concept, and a person is likely to have multiple identities based on gender, race, disability, and other statuses. Some identities are more salient than others. For some people, their disability might be their most salient identity, whereas for others, their disability may be less important than identities based on their familial, occupational, racial, religious, or ethnic statuses. These other identities may in fact be highly valued, both by the individual and by others in society, overshadowing any focus on disability as a primary identity. As M. W. Murugami (2009) and others have noted, some people with disabilities do not include their disabilities in their identities at all. The salience of a disability identity may be associated to some extent with its visibility, but salience tends to be situational. Identity salience, like identity content, is learned by interacting in social settings.

In summary, identity development occurs in the course of social interaction, primarily through interactions with significant others.

Because interaction continues to occur throughout the life course, identities are not static. Entering a new situation, particularly at a turning point in one's life, may result in identity change.

Identity as Process

The following account illustrates a change in disability identity as a result of an encounter with new significant others:

> Growing up, I wanted to dis-identify myself with the image or label of being a cripple. I wanted to be normal. . . . I avoided other disabled people. I refused to see myself as part of that group. . . . I drank excessively, consumed drugs and cigarettes, acted out my anger in violent outbursts, ended up in jails and hospitals. Finally, through some mysterious grace, I woke up and found myself in the company of an excellent therapist. . . .
>
> I joined a group of disabled women on the advice of my therapist. I hated the idea, but to my surprise they were marvelous, dynamic women. They shared so many of what I had always thought were my own isolated, personal experiences that I began to realize that my supposedly private hell was a social phenomenon. . . . Later on, . . . I felt pride and a sense of identity. (Tollifson 1997, 106–111)

For this woman, her encounters with the therapist and the group of disabled women served as turning points that led to identity change. C. Thomas (1999b, 53) described a different kind of turning point:

> [In this job] it was the first time I had had any contact with people with other disabilities and I benefited a lot by talking about my own experiences and listening to theirs. I suddenly wasn't on my own. They all seemed proud to be disabled and it was a part of them and for the first time I realized that I was who I was because of my disability and that it could be a positive thing.

Turning points may result in either positive or negative identity change. A study of men with AIDS transitioning to work showed that the men developed "anticipatory identities" of themselves as workers prior to entering the labor market (Ghaziani 2004). Personal experiences with stigma and discrimination, however, along with the complexities of the workplace, prevented the actualization of these anticipatory identities, resulting often in a change from self-efficacy to shame. Thus, self-concept development and identity formation are ongoing processes that continue throughout the life course as individuals encounter new situations and new definitions from significant others.

Situational Identity

Not only do actual identities change over time, but also individuals may *choose* to present themselves as having different identities, depending on the situation. Goffman (1959) describes the process of "presentation of self," during which individuals, like actors on a stage, attempt to project an image of themselves that may differ from their actual self-concept. For example, people with invisible disabilities may try to pass as "normal" by avoiding behaviors that would reveal their disability or by avoiding the use of "stigma symbols," such as white canes. Most people with disabilities use a variety of "impression management" strategies to negotiate potentially uncomfortable social situations.

Hidden disabilities may be especially problematic in social interaction. On the one hand, attempting to pass may be stressful because of the constant fear of disclosure, and passing may lower self-esteem if the person comes to see him- or herself as deceitful or dishonest. On the other hand, M. F. Olney and K. F. Brockelman (2003, 44) and others point out that when those with invisible disabilities present themselves honestly, they may not be believed. As one of their respondents said, "It's harder because people think that you're making it up."

Olney and Brockelman argue that passing is often a pragmatic decision rather than an indication of shame or stigma acceptance. In a study of students with psychiatric and cognitive disabilities, they have found that most of their interviewees had no desire for a "cure," but, at the same time, they were aware of the disadvantages of disclosure such as being stereotyped or labeled incompetent. Thus, they often had to decide what to reveal and to whom. The authors write, "Our analyses revealed that perception management is a sophisticated strategy used to minimise negative consequences while assuring appropriate accommodations" (2003, 48).

Passing is typically situational. As I show in Chapter 8, children and young adults with disabilities commonly use a variety of impression management strategies, including passing, to facilitate social participation. They may choose to emphasize their disabilities when they want special privileges at home or at school but may try to minimize or hide them when they want to "fit in" with nondisabled peers. Individuals who hide their disabilities when interacting with nondisabled others may switch to a disabled identity when they are with others with disabilities. Such identity switching may be resented by those with "full-time" disability identities, as this comment suggests: "I find it hard to embrace as brothers and sisters those folks who spend their whole lives comfortably in the nondisabled world without any mention of personal disability until a disabled person challenges their authority to speak for us" (Gill 1994, 46).

A. Asch (1984, 552) argues that the decision about self-presentation is sometimes imposed on people with disabilities by others in society. She claims that her blindness might have been an "inconsequential part of [her]self and [her] life," except that others have emphasized that aspect of her self and have expected her to speak for disabled people as a category. She relates an experience in a group dynamics program exercise, in which she had to choose whether to stand under a sign based on her gender, religion, age, race, or disability. She chose the disability sign because no one else in the program had a known disability and she thought it was important to represent that category—even though other aspects of her self-concept might have been more salient to her.

Thus, disability identity has a temporal component. Identities change as one moves from one social situation to another, often depending on what is acceptable or preferred in a particular group. Identity, then, is a social construction. At any point in time, individuals may have been exposed to a variety of definitions and appraisals of themselves as disabled. The definitions and appraisals that become salient during that situation depend on (1) the individual's preexisting definitions and appraisals of self and of disability, (2) the significance of the others present in the situation, (3) the perceived definitions of disability and appraisals of the individual held by the others in the situation, and (4) the importance of the situation for the individual. In some cases, a disability identity may compete with other identities, both positive and negative, for salience. In Chapter 4, I focus on the situation in which an individual has more than one potentially negative identity.

Conclusion

Looking-glass self theory in sociology suggests that individuals with disabilities who encounter negative definitions of themselves will internalize those definitions. Although early, often poorly designed studies suggested that such individuals do in fact have low self-esteem, more recent studies show considerable variability in self-esteem in this population, perhaps as a consequence of the increasing availability of diverse definitions in society. On a micro level, this variability can be explained by interactional conditions, such as the significance of the other providing the definition and the frequency of encountering the definition. As individuals age, they are likely to be exposed to new interactional situations and new definitions of themselves. As a result, self-esteem and disability identity are not static. In addition, individuals may *choose* to present themselves differently in different social situations, so that one's self-concept and presented self are not necessarily the same.

4

Intersecting Identities Among Women and African Americans with Disabilities

Disability identity is but one of a constellation of identities within the self-concept of a person with a disability. Along with his or her disability status, a person also holds gender, racial, ethnic, and other statuses. In some cases, disability may be the only socially devalued status a person holds. For example, a white man with a disability might face discrimination because of his disability but not on other grounds. An African American woman with a disability, however, might encounter stigma as a result of her race, gender, or disability, and the effect of that stigma might be multiplied by the number of devalued statuses she holds. The literature includes a growing number of studies that explore the interactions between devalued statuses, such as being gay or lesbian, a woman, or a member of a minority racial or ethnic community, and disability. Most of this literature has focused on women and African Americans with disabilities, groups that typify the issues involved in holding more than one devalued status. In this chapter I explore the effects of gender and race on disability identity, although they are certainly not the only statuses that interact with it.

A number of issues arise in connection with having multiple identities, including (1) salience, or the overshadowing of one identity by another; (2) conflict, which may occur when the goals of one membership group are in opposition to those of another; and (3) combination, or the multiplied effect of experiencing more than one stigma.

Salience

C. Bell (2011a) argues, using examples from the media, that black-ness is typically emphasized over disability in descriptions of African Americans with disabilities, reflecting a cultural focus on race over disability status. Some writers (see, e.g., citations in Vernon 1999) have suggested that the primacy of racism in society creates a situa-tion in which black people with disabilities have more in common with nondisabled blacks than they do with white people with disabil-ities. This suggestion implies that racial identity would be more salient than disability identity in the case of African Americans with disabilities. However, others have noted that disabled African Amer-icans may experience stigma from nondisabled African Americans (Vernon 1999), and K. E. McDonald and colleagues (2007) suggest that disabilities may isolate people from their racial/ethnic group, which might lead them to choose to associate with other people with disabilities, regardless of their race.

The nature of a disability also may play a role in salience for members of different racial and ethnic groups. As I showed in the lit-erature review in Chapter 2, some disabilities are more stigmatized than others, and ethnic groups vary in their attitudes toward different disabilities. Thus, a person with a disability that is especially deval-ued in his or her group might choose to de-emphasize disability iden-tity in favor of ethnic identity. The visibility of a disability may also play a role. McDonald and colleagues (2007) note that people with learning disabilities or other hidden disabilities may be more likely to choose a less concealable racial/ethnic identity over their disability identity.

Another important factor in salience might be timing. T. Shake-speare (cited in Whitney 2006) found that individuals identified more strongly with the community they joined first in life. In his study, people who identified themselves as gay or lesbian from an early age and who became disabled later in life continued to con-sider themselves primarily gay or lesbian rather than disabled. Peo-ple who are born with their disabilities or who acquire them early in life may have stronger disability identities than those who acquire their disabilities later in life. Timing, of course, would not play a role in salience in the case of race or gender coupled with congeni-tal disability.

Questions about salience arise with regard to gender. For women, family identities, especially the identity of mother, tend to be salient.

However, as S. N. Barnartt (2001) and others have suggested, disability can be a *master status* that affects all the other statuses held by a person. I am not aware of any large-scale empirical research that has looked directly at the salience of disability identity in relation to gender identity in women with disabilities, but researchers could use a measure of self-concept like the Twenty Statements Test (Kuhn and McPartland 1954) with women with disabilities to determine whether their disability or their gender was more salient to them.

Yet, as I suggested in Chapter 3, the self is situationally variable. Although a particular identity might be salient at any given time, a different identity might prevail at another. In describing the findings from her interview with an African American woman with a disability, A. Petersen (2006, 730) writes, "In coming to know and understand Krissy it occurred to me that she had little choice but to negotiate these conflicting identities. Like a chameleon, she accentuated one identity while downplaying or denying another. It was how she survived."

Conflict

M. Minow (1997) argues that identity politics tend to ignore "intersectionality," or the fact that all individuals belong to more than one group. Sometimes, these groups have competing interests, creating issues for social movement participation. Studies cited in McDonald et al. (2007, 147) and elsewhere have suggested that "focusing on multiple minority statuses may detract from advancing the cause of any one such status." As McDonald has written, "to fight for the rights of black people is one thing; to fight for the rights of disabled people is something else, [*sic*] there is not enough time and energy to fight two different wars" (cited in Vernon 1999, 391).

With regard to this situation, A. Vernon (1999, 391) asks, "which aspect of your identity do you prioritise and which do you leave out?" She argues that the choice is made more difficult by the fact that movements have been "monistic," or focused only on a single oppression. For example, the experience of disabled women has not been a priority of the women's movement, and the disability movement has not focused on the special concerns of women with disabilities (see, e.g., Lloyd 1992). L. A. Habib (1995, 50) notes a comment made in response to a suggestion that women's issues be included in the agenda of the disability movement: "The disability movement is already divided, and you are proposing a segregation that will weaken it even further." The alternative of creating a separate organization for a doubly stigmatized group like disabled women creates issues of its own. M. Lloyd (1992) notes that "the cold winds of separatism" may pose an even greater threat to an already marginalized minority.

In some cases, choosing an identity may be made more difficult by rejection by *both* marginalized groups. C. Whitney (2006) found, in a study of disabled women who also identified as queer, that some of the women felt they were rejected by the queer community because of their disabilities and also by the disability community because they were lesbians. This lack of community support might result in failure to identify with either community.

Some individuals may choose to prioritize what they see as their most oppressed status, as the following quote suggests: "Disability is the primary problem in our lives. Once we identify ourselves as powerful disabled individuals, we can go back into our secondary communities, whether it is to be the black community, the Chicano community, the women's community, or some combination of these" (Saxton and Howe, cited in Lloyd 1992, 208).

Although this issue is most likely to arise among politically active individuals, role conflict may occur in other situations as well. For example, in their discussion of "sexism without the pedestal," M. Fine and A. Asch (1981) argue that an inherent conflict exists between the traditional "pampered" role assigned to women and the stigma of disability. Although these roles are changing in modern society, the continued existence of stereotypical views could result in difficult choices regarding which role to play or which identity to emphasize.

Combination

Do individuals with two devalued identities experience double the stigma of those with only one such identity? Vernon notes possibilities such as "double jeopardy," "triple disadvantage," and "simultaneous oppression." She cites this passage as an example:

> Whenever the subject of race came up at home, someone would remind me that as a black person who is also disabled, my chances of achieving anything in life were probably less than zero. It was

my "destiny" to suffer twice as much discrimination and to miss twice as many opportunities as the person who is "only black" or "only disabled." (McDonald, quoted in Vernon 1999, 387)

A disabled woman wrote this about the problem of meeting others' expectations on the job: "I work [in] a male dominated environment. I do feel that I have had to be four times as good as the men to be accepted—I am a woman and also disabled" (Thomas 1999a, 53).

Multiple identities are likely to interact in complex ways, not necessarily resulting in disadvantage that is an exact multiple of the number of identities in question. McDonald and colleagues (2007) suggest that the experience of being a "minority within a minority" may have a number of dimensions, based on factors such as the nature of a disability. The interaction of multiple devalued identities has received greater attention in the literature in the cases of disabled women and African Americans with disabilities. I explore these cases further in the sections below.

Women with Disabilities

Double Oppression?

A number of articles on women with disabilities have used terms like "two handicaps plus" (Hanna and Rogovsky 1991) and "double discrimination" (Habib 1995) to suggest that disadvantage is multiplied. M. J. Deegan (1985, 39) describes women with physical disabilities as a "multiple minority group" that experiences differential and unequal treatment that is "more severely limiting" than that applied to a single minority group. She writes, "Multiple minorities are the most disenfranchised members of society" because of the interaction effect of their statuses (40). W. J. Hanna and B. Rogovsky (1991) point to several statistical indicators of the disadvantaged status of disabled women. They are less likely to marry, likely to have less education, and less likely to be employed than either nondisabled women or disabled men. In a study based on more recent data from large samples, L. Schur (2004) found that women with disabilities continue to have lower employment and income levels and higher poverty rates than men with disabilities or nondisabled women. They also tend to be more socially isolated.

Habib (1995) argues that in developing countries especially, women with disabilities tend to be marginalized and isolated. Boylan (cited in Habib 1995, 50) writes of this population, "Disability diminishes sharply their often inferior roles, even in their own households. The stigma of disability, with its myths and fears, increases their social isolation. When no rehabilitation facilities are available, they become immobile and housebound, and their isolation is complete." Habib notes that, in comparison with disabled men in developing countries, women with disabilities are more likely to be poor and to have difficulty in obtaining services. They also are more likely to experience physical, sexual, and psychological abuse. These experiences are probably related to the cultural stereotypes and role prescriptions that are assigned to women in most of the world.

Cultural Roles and Stereotypes

Although gender roles have been changing in modern society, traditionally women were expected to be (1) physically attractive (according to the norms of the society in which they lived), (2) nurturing (in order to play the role of caregiver for other family members), and (3) dependent (on men for their livelihood and safety). Each of these role prescriptions has been problematic for women with disabilities.

Physical attractiveness. According to Hanna and Rogovsky (1991, 56) "few men think of a visibly disabled woman as a sex object." Part of the problem lies in contemporary standards of beauty: "The media sex symbol of the day is an impossible standard for any woman to live up to, but disability places you at an even greater disadvantage. If you spend most of your time in a wheelchair . . . , no matter what you do, you're not going to look like Cheryl Tiegs or Marilyn Monroe" (Bogle and Shaul, cited in Hanna and Rogovsky 1991, 57). Hanna and Rogovsky present survey results showing that the term *woman* is associated with beauty, whereas the term *disabled woman* evokes negative associations such as "ugly" and "unpleasant."

Fine and Asch (1988) note that the feminine norm in our culture includes bodily integrity, grace, and ease and that men value physical attractiveness in a partner more than women do. Thus, heterosexual women with visible disabilities are disadvantaged in their quest for relationships with men and are less likely to have a partner than their nondisabled counterparts.

In a qualitative study of women with disabilities, H. Zitzelsberger (2005) found that her respondents often engaged in impression management techniques such as passing in order to minimize the appearance of their bodily differences. Not all her respondents were seen as unattractive, however, and one noted that people were surprised by her attractiveness because she used a scooter: "I get comments from strangers all the time and it has to do with the combination of being young, and being in a scooter. . . . They'll comment on how I'm young and they'll say, 'Oh, you know, you're beautiful, it's too bad' . . . They would always make comments about my looks and my having a disability and how that can't be" (395). This example illustrates the perceived incompatibility between disability and physical attractiveness by showing how an attractive disabled woman is believed to be an "exception."

Nurturance, caregiving, and dependence. Women's gender roles have traditionally included the expectation that women will be the family caregivers. This expectation becomes problematic in the case of women with disabilities, who may need care themselves. M. Blackwell-Stratton and colleagues (1988, 307) argue that disabled women experience "rolelessness." They are restricted from playing the socially sanctioned roles of wife and mother and are also denied the role of independent adult; instead, "a disabled person is like an eternal poster child, cute but not sexy; always the cared for, never the caring."

K. Barron (1997) cites cases of disabled women who were not taught to cook or perform other household chores by their mothers, even though they had expressed a desire to learn. Fine and Asch (1988, 17) raise a question that a man might pose: "How can she minister to his needs when a disabled woman epitomizes all that is needy herself?" The same question is likely to be raised in the case of a disabled woman who is or wants to be a mother. Fine and Asch note that women with disabilities commonly face discrimination in adoption and child custody cases as a result of the perception that they are not fit caregivers.

In their study of verbal associations, Hanna and Rogovsky (1991) report that the term *woman* was associated with terms like *married, mom,* and *child bearer.* The role of mother may, in fact, be the most central expectation associated with women's place in society. Yet *disabled woman* rarely elicited such associations. Hanna and Rogovsky's respondents reported that they were advised by physicians and family members not to have children, and those who did have children reported being told that they should not have done so.

These stereotypes are often linked to an assumption that women with disabilities lack sexuality: "The rights to marriage, to sexual and reproductive rights, and to family life are often implicitly denied to disabled women on the basis that disability has deprived them of their sexuality and they can therefore no longer fulfill the roles of sexual partner, mother and carer" (Habib 1995, 51). Barron (1997) cites as an example of their perceived asexuality the cases of young women with disabilities who were asked by men whether they needed help in going to the bathroom. Lloyd (1992) argues that the sexuality of disabled women is constructed in "disablist" rather than sexist terms, paralleling the racist construction of black women's sexuality.

In a study of stereotypes using both disabled and nondisabled respondents, (Nario-Redmond 2010), nondisabled men and women were described very differently from each other, but people with disabilities, regardless of gender, were described as unattractive, dependent, incompetent, and asexual. Disabled women shared few descriptors with their nondisabled counterparts. Although both disabled and nondisabled women were described as weak and incompetent, disabled women were never labeled feminine and were only rarely considered nurturing, and, in keeping with the findings of other studies noted above, they were nearly universally seen as unfit parents. Interestingly, results were similar for disabled and nondisabled respondents, suggesting that people with disabilities are socialized to accept the same stereotypes as others in society (although the research does not suggest that they accept them or use them in their self-appraisals). The relative recency of Nario-Redmond's study (2010) suggests that role expectations for disabled women have not changed much since earlier studies.

These studies suggest that both women and people with disabilities have been expected to be passive and dependent. Yet some women defy these expectations. H. Meekosha (2002) argues that a feminist disability rights movement in Australia provides a venue for disabled women to gain independence. She quotes a movement activist who says, "Many women with disabilities experience in their lives an enormous degree of lack of agency, lack of autonomy, lack of faith of other people and themselves in their own decision-making capacity . . . so having an organization which is run by women with disabilities . . . is enormous, and an enormously empowering thing" (68). Similarly, Barron (1997, 27) argues that taking part in a social movement such as the disability rights movement enables disabled women to overcome expectations of passivity and dependence. "By opposing the traditional understanding of appropriate behaviour not only for 'the disabled' but also for women, the young women are attempting to take control of their lives." However, as Nario-Redmond's results above suggest, the preponderance of stereotypical thinking, even in today's society, may limit opportunities for empowerment.

Portrayals of Disabled Women in the Media

Blackwell-Stratton and colleagues (1988) point to two televised events that typify the images of women and of people with disabilities in the media: the Miss America Pageant and telethons. They argue that the beauty queen represents the ideal of physical perfection that many women strive to achieve, whereas the poster child in need of a cure represents what is least desired by expectant parents.

After reviewing numerous novels about women with disabilities, D. Kent (1988, 93) concludes that they are remarkably similar in their depictions of disabled women: "Whether she is blind or deaf, facially disfigured or paraplegic, the disabled woman is typically shown to be incomplete not only in body, but in the basic expression of her womanhood." Kent cites examples such as Laura in *The Glass Menagerie* and Edith in *The Bleeding Heart*. Most are portrayed as victims and as dependent on others, and the majority express bitterness, despair, and self-loathing. Yet they do not rebel against society's view of them as useless, pitiable, and undesirable.

Similarly, disabled women are presented in stereotypical ways in the movies. M. A. Cahill and M. F. Norden (2003, 59) note that women with disabilities only rarely appear in films, and when they do, they typically have disabilities such as blindness or deafness that do not adversely affect their appearance. When disabled women have been depicted in films, they have generally fallen into a few narrow categories: "the ingénue-victim, the awe-inspiring overachiever, the defender-avenger, the comical or horrible repellent, and the novelty." The first two categories have been the most common by far.

As Cahill and Norden point out, the disabled woman is usually cured by the end of the film or, at least, has managed to overcome her disability and resume "normal" activities. They argue that these movies convey the message that "it is virtually impossible for women to be both average and disabled" (2003, 73). Thus, as role models, these characters suggest that unless women with disabilities are "inspirational," they are unattractive and unacceptable. With regard to these Hollywood portrayals, the authors ask, "Where is the profoundly disabled woman whose disability is congenital and deforming? Where is the disabled fat woman? . . . Everywhere in the world, but not in Hollywood film" (74). Although some newer portrayals on television and in the movies have been more realistic, in general, stereotypes have prevailed.

Such stereotypical depictions appear to play a role in the development of self-esteem in girls and women with disabilities. D. Kent (1988) cites studies showing that young women tend to identify with female characters in literature. Characters from books and film and television become part of young women's reference groups, along with people they know face-to-face. In the next section I consider how disabled women are affected by cultural views of women with disabilities.

Effects on Self and Identity

Many girls with disabilities are socialized from an early age to accept the stereotypes that are prevalent in society, and these appear to be internalized. As I noted in Chapter 3, women with disabilities tend to have lower self-esteem and lower perceived quality of life scores than other women. Similarly, Hanna and Rogovsky (1991, 59) note that self-esteem is comparatively low among women in general and especially low among women with disabilities. One of their respondents comments, "Disabled women have a self-image that accepts the image the rest of the world has: that they cannot do, and they shouldn't even attempt to do." Their respondents also reported receiving verbal and nonverbal messages from their significant others that reflected the sexism and ableism of the larger society. Similarly, Schur (2004) has found that women with disabilities reported lower levels of life satisfaction and role fulfillment than women and men without disabilities. Interestingly though, she did not find significant differences in these measures between disabled women and disabled men.

Disabled women seem to accept normative role expectations, including those related to physical beauty and heterosexual relationships. S. Hannaford (cited in Gerschick 2000, 1266) explains, "I discovered on becoming officially defined as 'disabled' that I lost my previous identity as a sexually attractive being." One of Zitzelsberger's (2005, 395) respondents remarks, "It is a constant struggle with your self-esteem and your feelings of who you are as a woman.

. . . You don't want to be regarded as a sex object but you want to be regarded as a sexual being." Similarly, Barron (1997) notes that one of her respondents felt that she was "worth something" only after having a relationship with a nondisabled man. None of her respondents could name any positive aspects of their physical appearances.

In a study of identity among people with disabilities, N. Watson (2002) found that most of his respondents had positive self-images. However, the small number who saw themselves negatively were all women. One said, "I think I look terrible . . . when I go to bed at night, I think, I wish I could just fall asleep and never face another day" (522). Another remarked, "I just feel that before everything happened things were good and boyfriends were on the scene and marriage was on the scene and everything changed with MS" (523). Both of these women subscribed to a medical model of disability and blamed themselves for their social isolation.

Thomas (1999a, 91) presents the case of a disabled woman who experienced negative reactions to her pregnancy from medical professionals, who believed she was not capable of being a good mother. As a result, she began to question her own abilities: "I've been through quite a lot of guilt in the early weeks of [my baby's] life that maybe they were right and I shouldn't have had a baby." Disabled women who repeatedly encounter such negative appraisals in their interactions with significant others are probably likely to internalize those appraisals and incorporate them into their self-concepts.

Fine and Asch (1988) suggest that low self-esteem among disabled women may be related to their rolelessness discussed earlier. Disabled girls learn that they should not aspire to the goals of physical beauty, caregiving, and sexuality that have been established for other women in society. As a result, they do not have clear norms within which to define themselves and may not be able to readily determine their self-worth. Unlike nondisabled girls, who typically have a convenient role model (their mother), disabled girls with nondisabled mothers may believe they need to look elsewhere for models of womanhood. Consequently, Fine and Asch argue, young women with disabilities may turn toward conventionally male standards of achievement, such as careers, to validate their self-concepts. Of course, opportunities for education and employment may be limited for them as well, preventing them from developing high self-esteem in this alternative way.

Negative self-views in disabled women appear to be associated with mental health issues such as depression and stress (Nosek and

Hughes 2003). J. P. Niemeier (2008) found in a sample of people undergoing rehabilitation that disabled women were more than twice as likely as disabled men to be depressed. Compared with men, women also reported more intense and different symptoms of grief and depression. The author concluded that gender was a risk factor for negative mental health outcomes following a disabling injury.

Although women with disabilities are clearly at risk for low self-esteem and mental health problems, many of them manage to avoid these issues. In a study of women with physical disabilities, H. M. DeKlerk and L. Ampousah (2003, 1136) found that their respondents usually felt good about themselves. These women did indicate that they were aware of negative societal views regarding disabled women, but "they had conditioned themselves not to be influenced by other people's viewpoints, especially when they do not even know these people." This finding suggests that these women had significant others who transmitted positive views to them and served as buffers against societal stigma.

Similarly, Fine and Asch (1988) cite cases of disabled women who manage to forge positive identities even though they have been exposed to gender- and disability-based stereotypes. In some cases, disability pride seems to develop even though family members do not promote it. For example, H. Rousso (1984) has written about her mother's attempts to get her to "walk straight," while she saw her uneven gait as a part of her identity that did not need to be changed. Her strong sense of self may have developed from other feedback she received during her early years.

In a study of queer women with disabilities, Whitney (2006) argues that identity development is a gradual process. She uses C. J. Gill's (1997) model of identity development to show how her respondents moved from denying their disabilities to embracing them as they encountered others with more positive views than those to which they had initially been exposed. As I noted in Chapter 3, disability pride tends to be an acquired self-view that emerges at turning points in life. However, my earlier research suggests that many, and perhaps most people with disabilities do not encounter such turning points and that disability pride may be an identity found in only a minority of people with disabilities (Darling and Heckert 2010a). Interestingly, we found that gender did not affect the nature of disability identity and that both pride and shame occurred among both men and women. I discuss our findings in depth in Chapter 7.

In summary, then, the literature suggests that, in general, women with disabilities tend to have more negative self-views than disabled men. These views appear to result from a combination of disability- and gender-based stereotypes to which women are exposed from an early age. However, many women are able to maintain positive self-views through exposure to alternative definitions from significant others. For some, these alternative definitions are available during childhood and adolescence; others may not encounter them until later in life.

African Americans with Disabilities

The literature on the identities of African Americans with disabilities is not as large as the literature on the identities of disabled women. Recently, this topic has received more attention than in the past (see, e.g., Bell 2011a), but many of these newer studies are based on literary analysis rather than on social science research. In a theoretical article based on psychological research, C. J. Gill and W. E. Cross (2010) note several points of convergence between black identity theory and disability identity: (1) the existential encounter with society's categorization of oneself as a member of a stigmatized group; (2) multiple patterns of socialization leading to black/disability identity; (3) no singular expression of black or disability identity; and (4) the importance of the enactment or expression of identity in everyday life. A review of the small number of studies of disability identity in African Americans suggests two common themes: simultaneous oppression and the salience of racial identity.

Simultaneous Oppression

Like women, African Americans with disabilities are subject to more than one oppression. However, some writers have suggested that the term *double oppression* does not adequately explain the situation of disabled African Americans.

> I reject the notion that black disabled people experience a kind of double oppression. . . . on the contrary, I suggest that racism within disability is part of a process of simultaneous oppression which black people experience daily in Western society. It is also an experience which divides disabled people from their black able-bodied peers. . . . because of this situation . . . it is necessary to construct a distinct and separate black disabled identity. (Stuart 1992, 179)

O. W. Stuart argues that simultaneous oppression is evidenced by an absence of cultural representations of black people with disabilities, even less access to resources than their nondisabled peers, and isolation within the black community.

Similarly, P. Block and colleagues (2002) show how society has explained race, poverty, and disability in the same terms—as products of individual failure. Such victim blaming has resulted in a self-fulfilling prophecy, as race, poverty, and disability have become linked through a lack of access to resources: "People living with multiple stigmas have limited opportunities and resources available to them and face societal barriers and oppression that result in poverty and exclusion" (Block et al. 2002, 37).

R. J. Alston and colleagues (1996, 13) also assert that racial and disability identity are inseparable in disabled African Americans. They cite an example from G. B. Anderson and C. Grace of a black, deaf, adolescent female who, when asked whether she identified more with the black community or the deaf community, replied, "I'm black deaf. My community is the black deaf community." They argue that such individuals have achieved an "integrated identity" that makes a choice between identities impossible: "For African Americans with disabilities, racial identity development does not occur in a vacuum . . . [it] occurs in the context of the disability" (13). The authors note that the simultaneous internalization of these two identities is most likely to occur among individuals who are disabled from birth, a likelihood also noted by E. Mpofu and D. A. Harley (2006); otherwise, a newly acquired disability might have the effect of interrupting black identity development. Yet members of racial minority groups might be better prepared for the stigma associated with a disability acquired later in life because they have already been exposed to racial stigma and have been socialized to adapt to the status of "outsider."

The Salience of Racial Identity

P. Devlieger and G. Albrecht (2000) argue that African Americans living in the inner city are not likely to identify with ideas like disability culture, disability rights, or disability pride because they need to focus on the struggles of everyday life:

> Disability is not the most critical life issue to inner-city African Americans, who daily face the more pressing problems of poverty; finding a place to live; feeding one's self and the children; guarding

one's security against gangs, violence, and drugs; and confronting racism, which often results in inadequate education, unemployment, and denied benefits. (p. 58)

Thus, disability identity as conceptualized by proponents of the social model, may lack salience or even be nonexistent in this population.

Moreover, negative stereotypes of disability persist in the culture of inner-city African American communities. M. Bailey (2011) notes that hip-hop music has included disability slurs like *retard* and *crazy*. She argues that devaluing members of a different minority group in this way serves as a means of managing racial stigma. Exposure to these slurs may reinforce negative stereotypes of disability in this community, further distancing its members from social model concepts like disability pride.

African Americans with disabilities may also have less access to the disability rights community. As S. V. King (1998) and others have noted, African American families sometimes shelter members with disabilities, denying them the opportunity to meet or interact with others who might expose them to alternative identities. She asserts, moreover, that disability has always been common in the African American community and that its members tend to believe they should take care of their own. Thus, the medical model has tended to prevail, and both King (1998) and Devlieger and Albrecht (2000) have cited examples of African Americans who either deny or lament their disabilities. However, socioeconomic status might be an important mediating variable; middle- or upper-class African Americans, especially those with higher levels of education, might be more likely to have been exposed to the tenets of the disability rights movement and the social model.

In general, these studies suggest that racial identity is more salient than disability identity in this community. This suggestion is supported by other writings noted earlier in this chapter that pointed to a low level of African American involvement in the disability rights movement. However, identity salience varies among individual members of a group.

A Typology of Identities

Mpofu and Harley (2006) suggest that the intersection of racial identity and disability identity produces four logical possibilities: (1) high racial identity/high disability identity, (2) high racial identity/low disability identity, (3) low racial identity/high disability identity, and (4) low racial identity/low disability identity. By "high racial identity," they mean black pride, or satisfaction with being African American. Similarly, "high disability identity" indicates disability pride. They argue, from a psychological perspective, that identity pride is healthier than its opposite, the internalization of societal stigma.

The typology suggested by Mpofu and Harley's identity levels merits further analysis. Table 4.1 provides a basis for considering each of the identity types. Each cell represents the intersection of the level of racial identity and disability identity in any given individual. These cells are ideal types, and actual identities may in fact form a continuum or be situational. However, to the extent that individuals more closely approximate one type than another, this typology may be useful in understanding the intersection of these two identities.

Black pride/disability pride. Individuals who approximate this type are likely to have had their disabilities since birth. As a result, they are less likely to have internalized negative stereotypes about disability that are present in the African American community, as well as in society as a whole. They may also have higher levels of education and access to the Internet, with consequent exposure to the disability rights/disability culture communities. Some of the prominent African American members of these communities in recent years, like Chris Bell, exemplify this type.

Race traitors. V. Kannen (2008) and others use the term *identity treason* to describe the behavior of privileged individuals (e.g., those who are white and nondisabled) who choose to identify with devalued groups (e.g., claiming blackness or disability). Here, I am using the term somewhat differently to describe members of a devalued group (African Americans or people with disabilities) who choose not to identify with their own group. In the proposed typol-

Table 4.1 A Typology of Identities Among African Americans with Disabilities

		Racial Identity	
		High	Low
Disability Identity	High	Black pride/disability pride	Race traitor
	Low	Disability traitor	Black shame/disability shame

ogy, a race traitor is a disabled African American who chooses to identify with the disability community rather than the African American community.

Such individuals may also have acquired a disability early in life, so that disability is central to their identity. Perhaps they have lived in an integrated or mostly white community or have been rejected by the black community—lowering the salience of their African American identity. Those who approximate this type may also be more highly educated or at least have been exposed to the tenets of the social model of disability.

Disability traitor. This category includes some of the inner-city African Americans described by Devlieger and Albrecht (2000) mentioned earlier in this chapter. These individuals have black pride but no positive identity as persons with disabilities. They espouse the medical model and, consequently, view their disabilities as tragedies or problems needing to be fixed. Such individuals are likely to be poor and not well educated, limiting their exposure to the disability rights/disability culture communities and to the social model.

Black shame/disability shame. This type is the polar opposite of black pride/disability pride. Individuals in this category are proud of neither their race nor their disability status. They might try to pass as white or as nondisabled. Variables associated with such a type include acquiring a disability later in life, after having internalized societal stigma and the tenets of the medical model. In addition, like the race traitors described above, these individuals may have been isolated from or rejected by the African American community.

As noted earlier, these ideal types only approximate the actual identities of African Americans with disabilities. Gill and Cross (2010) and others have described a wide range of identity variation in this population, including "assimilationist," "humanist," and other ways of thinking about identity. As I will show in Chapter 6, identity divesity may characterize the entire population of people with disabilities.

Conclusion

As I have shown in this chapter, identities interact in complex ways. Individuals with multiple devalued statuses may choose to identify with any or none of those statuses. Clearly, those who are members of other devalued groups in addition to having disabilities must contend with greater oppression and more stereotyping than those who are "only" disabled. However, those oppressions are not simple multiples of one another. The issues raised by multiple devalued identities include salience, or the relative importance of each identity; conflict, or the extent to which the promotion of one identity may interfere with the promotion or enactment of another, and combination, or the nature of interactions among the identities in question.

Several variables appear to play a role in determining identity choice and response to oppression, including the nature of the disability, the definitions received from significant others, and exposure to the medical and social models. Further research is needed to elucidate the complex relationships among gender, race, and disability identities.

5

The Disability
Rights Movement and
Identity Politics

In Chapters 2, 3, and 4 I focused on stigma and the effects of negative societal views on self-concept and identity. In this chapter, I explore the changing views of disability since the 1970s and will look at how these more positive views have been associated with newer self-views like disability pride. The impetus for much of this change has been the disability rights movement, which led to the passage of the Americans with Disabilities Act in the United States and similar legislation in other countries. The movement has raised public awareness of disability rights issues and has promoted new, more positive images of people with disabilities in the media, although older images continue to exist (see, e.g., Haller et al. 2006).

In this chapter, I briefly review the history of the disability rights movement in the United States and its association with identity politics, followed by a discussion of recent psychological theories of disability identity development that have arisen in the wake of the movement. Finally, using a sociological perspective, I present a model of disability identity development that explains disability pride as well as other types of disability identity.

The Disability Rights Movement

In the past, people with disabilities living at home were commonly isolated from one another. Prior to the passage of the ADA, physical barriers in the environment, such as a lack of curb cuts and inaccessible buses, made freedom of movement difficult, and prior to the emergence of technological advances such as computers that "speak," individuals with some types of impairments were unable to easily communicate with others. Stigma and shame made normal social interaction problematic and kept many people with disabilities homebound. As a result, the medical or individual model of disability prevailed, and many disabled people did not recognize that others shared their plight. Furthermore, the helplessness that was commonly part of the disabled role was incompatible with activism to bring about social change. Finally, unlike members of racial and ethnic minority groups, people with disabilities commonly grew up in families in which other members were not disabled, so the development of a shared identity could not occur until they left home or encountered others like themselves. Given all these barriers, the actions of a few disability rights pioneers, as early as the 1930s, are quite remarkable.

P. K. Longmore (2003) describes the emergence of the League of the Physically Handicapped, a small group of disabled activists who protested job discrimination during the Depression. However, this group was something of an anomaly in its time, and widespread, organized activism did not develop until several decades later. As Longmore notes, most early disability activism grew out of friendship networks that developed in residential schools, where people with disabilities had access to others like themselves. The Deaf culture movement and advocacy for Deaf self-determination flourished at Gallaudet University and coalesced into the "Deaf President Now" movement of the 1980s (Shapiro 1994). Single-disability organizations like the National Association of the Deaf and the National Federation of the Blind were also early leaders in the disability rights movement.

An important impetus for disability activism was the civil rights movements of the 1950s and 1960s. African Americans and women provided models for organizing on behalf of minority rights. H. McCarthy (2003) notes that leaders of the emerging disability rights movement in the 1960s were influenced by other civil rights movements. One of the most influential of these emerging movements was the independent living movement, which grew out of a culture of student activism at the University of California at Berkeley in the late 1960s and early 1970s (Longmore 2003).

Meetings that brought together leaders of several emerging disability rights organizations also encouraged the movement to grow. R. Scotch (1988) cites networking opportunities provided by annual meetings of the President's Commission on Employment of the Handicapped in the early 1970s. These meetings were important in promoting cross-disability interaction, leading to a shared awareness that individuals with different impairments faced common issues of stigma and discrimination. By the late 1970s, these activists were organizing protests in Washington, D.C., and elsewhere to demand enforcement of current disability rights laws like Section 504 of the Rehabilitation Act of 1973 and, later, to bring about the passage of the ADA in 1990. With respect to the fight for passage of the ADA, Shapiro (1994, 126–127) cites this statement by a movement leader: "People with epilepsy will now be advocates for the same piece of legislation as people who are deaf. That has never happened before."

In interviews with leaders in the disability rights movement, McCarthy (2003) found that many of his respondents attributed their involvement to encounters with early movement leaders at national conferences. Meeting these role models encouraged them to organize their own communities or to engage in protests or other forms of activism. As one respondent said,

> That was the turning point for me—when I met Judy Heumann and Ed Roberts. They acted and spoke like there was nothing wrong with them; that what was wrong was that the doors were too narrow. . . . When they articulated that the problem was not them . . . and that because of social and environmental conditions, they were somehow disenfranchised—just like Black people had been—and put on the outside, that was an enormous relief to me. . . . It redefined me, or helped me redefine myself. (McCarthy 2003, 217–218)

The growth of the movement was further fueled by increasing opportunities for interaction brought about by technological advances and the mandated elimination of barriers resulting from newer legislation, such as the ADA and the Individuals with Disabilities Education Act. In particular, the increasing availability of the Internet enabled many individuals with disabilities to connect with others for the first time. However, as K. Dobransky and E. Hargittai (2006) have noted, socioeconomic status continues to be an important determinant of computer use among people with disabilities, and those of higher status are more likely than those with fewer resources to have access to the Internet and, consequently, to the tenets of the disability rights movement and the social model.

Today, the disability rights movement has taken its place alongside other civil rights movements as an institutionalized organization

promoting pride in a minority identity. An announcement for the Annual West Coast Disability Pride Parade and Festival recalls similar
events organized by African Americans, gays and lesbians, and other
minorities to showcase their successful struggles and identities:

> the puppet is an artistic representation of the late Justin Dart, a pio-
> neering advocate of the ADA . . . and [will] make its debut appear-
> ance in the [parade]. Matrix's giant puppet heroes are created to
> bring light to those who were on the forefront of civil rights, envi-
> ronmentalism, and played a major part within the community.
> Three leading women in the disability rights movement will serve
> as the parade's Grand Marshalls. (SDS Discussion List 2011)

Although many activists do not participate in such events, their existence suggests a new openness about a once-downplayed identity.

Longmore (2003, 114) summarizes the principles of the independent living movement and of the disability rights movement in
general:

- The reframing of "disability" as a social and political, rather
  than simply a medical and rehabilitative, problem.
- The shift in priorities from correcting individuals to reforming
  society.
- The assertion that the necessary means for social participation
  and integration, whether devices and services or access and accommodations, should be enforceable civil rights rather than
  dispensations of charity.
- The contests for power with professionals and bureaucrats.
- The quest for both individual and collective empowerment and
  self-determination.

In a similar vein, M. Putnam (2005, 191–197) states that "political disability identity" has the following components:

- Self-worth: the beliefs that one's worth is the same as that of
  those without disabilities, that one can be a productive member
  of society, and that persons with disabilities are undervalued in
  society.
- Pride/claiming disability: the belief that disability is a common
  human condition; the belief that impairment is not inherently
  negative; and the recognition that one belongs to a cultural minority group.

- Discrimination: the beliefs that people with disabilities are negatively stereotyped, that people with disabilities are typically treated differently, and that discrimination results in inequality of opportunity.
- Common cause: the beliefs that persons with disabilities share similar experiences, that some of these experiences should be changed, that the causes of these experiences are similar, and that there is a need for a common political agenda.
- Policy alternatives: the beliefs that disability is not characteristic of the individual, that contributors to the disability experience can be identified and addressed, and that opportunities are influenced by public policy.
- Engagement in political action: people with disabilities are a political constituency group; disability constituency groups represent political minority groups; and engagement in political action can effect policy change.

J. Swain and S. French (2000) use the term *affirmation* to describe the collective and personal identities that have emerged from disability culture and the disability rights movement. These identities are part of an affirmation model of disability that is replacing the older tragedy model.

Identity Politics and Personal Identity

Clearly, identity and activism have been linked in the ideology of the disability rights movement. R. R. Anspach (1979, 765) was one of the first to use the concept of identity politics to refer to social movements that "seek to alter the self-conceptions and societal conceptions of their participants." By locating the source of participants' problems in an inequitable social structure rather than in the participants themselves, the disability rights movement challenged prevailing negative self-views and replaced them with more positive ones. In support of theoretical arguments suggesting an association between disability pride and involvement in disability rights activism, a recent empirical study using two samples of people with disabilities found that "those who claimed disability as a central aspect of their identity were more likely to value their disability experiences, express community pride, and advocate for social change"(Nario-Redmond et al. 2011, 18).

A number of writers have described similar processes of redefinition of the self in a variety of recent social movements, including the women's movement, the gay rights movement, and others. M. Berbrier (2002), for example, notes that the African American civil rights movement played an important role in changing the perceived connotation of *minority group* from victimhood to empowerment. He argues that this change served as a means of *stigma transformation* that removed the deviance from the label and, in turn, "normalized" the identity of a category of people. He states further that the new identity norms associated with the multiculturalism of the late twentieth century enabled other previously stigmatized groups, including gay and deaf people, to change their collective identities. Similarly, Bernstein (2005) uses Michel Foucault's term *reverse affirmation* to describe the destigmatization of labels by social movements through the process of identity politics.

Berbrier (2002) suggests that the transformation of stigmatized identities through social movements is a form of "stigma management" (Goffman 1963), but Bailey (2011) argues that stigma management may actually be a barrier to identity politics because it assumes a need to normalize a devalued attribute. Indeed, many disability activists would argue that normalization is not the goal of their movements; rather, they celebrate their difference from the norm and see it as a form of positive deviance.

Various criticisms have developed in response to identity politics in general and political disability identity in particular. Some have questioned the premise of identity politics and argued that the acceptance of an identity created by an oppressive society only reinforces socially imposed segregation (Thomas 1999a; Alcoff and Mohanty 2006). R. Galvin (2003, 682) writes, "By claiming an identity which has been created through the processes of hierarchical differentiation and exclusion, subjugated peoples reinforce their own oppression," and M. Minow (1997, 57) adds, "dwelling on historic harm saps energy for new living." M. J. Piore (cited in Cerulo 1997) argues that identity politics isolates one community from another rather than creating a shared commitment to a unified national structure. Others (Siebers 2006) have asserted that the social constructionist basis of identity politics is flawed because it downplays the reality of lived experience. Minow (1997) also points out that focusing on a single identity tends to reinforce stereotyping and to downplay the multiplicity of identities that characterize every individual. And at a recent lecture I attended, noted author Salman Rushdie contended that identity politics are limiting because focusing on a single identity narrows one's scope and having a broad range of identities creates more options and life choices. These and other critiques may change the nature of identity politics in the future. As these ideas continue to evolve, the identities created by social movements are likely to change. However, the identity of disability pride that emerged from the disability rights movement in the late twentieth century still appears to be gaining momentum in today's world.

The National Organization of Disability/Harris Survey of Americans with Disabilities (National 2000) documents the growth of a sense of common identity among people with disabilities. In 1986, 40 percent of the people with disabilities in their national sample identified somewhat or strongly with the disabled population, and in 2000, 47 percent shared a sense of common identity with people with disabilities. As the data suggest, however, more than half of those surveyed did *not* share this identity, and Putnam (2005), L. Schur (2004), and others have noted that only a small number of people with disabilities are politically active. The survey also showed that a sense of common identity was more prevalent among people with severe impairments than among those with slight impairments. (See Chapter 6 for further consideration of this diversity in attitudes.)

By promoting a collective identity, social movements can shape the personal identities of their members, as well as those of nonmembers who become aware of the movement's message. However, as Putnam (2005) asserts, the process through which a political disability identity becomes internalized has received little research attention. This question is addressed to some extent in the work of psychologist Carol Gill.

Gill (1997; Gill and Cross 2010) rejects a medical model of identity development that is based on a need to "overcome" one's disability in order to fit in with "normal" society. Instead, she posits a sequential model of disability identity development based on four types of integration: (1) coming to feel we belong (integrating into society), (2) coming home (integrating with the disability community), (3) coming together (internally integrating our sameness and "differentness"), and (4) coming out (integrating how we feel with how we present ourselves) (Gill 1997, 42–45). She writes, "The 'coming out' process is often the last step toward disability identity in a path that begins with a desire to find a place in society, continues with a discovery of one's place in a community of peers, and builds to an appreciation and acceptance of one's whole self complete with disability" (Gill 1997, 45).

Gill's model has been used in a number of studies of disability identity development. Carol Gill and W. E. Cross Jr. (2010), and E. Mpofu and D. A. Harley (2006) have noted parallels between the development of racial identity and disability identity. Mpofu and Harley suggest that coming out, especially in a political way, is a higher stage of identity development than acceptance of societal stigma and results in higher self-esteem. However, as I show in Chapter 6, high self-esteem and life satisfaction may be associated with more than one type of disability identity. C. Whitney (2006) found that for some of the queer women with disabilities she interviewed, identity development was a gradual process. For some, coming home was facilitated by connecting with others through the Internet. Many began to come out as a disabled person when, as students, they encountered disabled activists and readings about disability identity. Whitney concludes that identities are likely to change as people encounter new life experiences, a finding that concurs with the tenets of symbolic interaction theory.

A Sociological Model of Disability Identity Development

As noted in earlier chapters, symbolic interaction theory has been concerned with the society-individual nexus. Through the mechanism of role-taking, the self-concept of an individual is shaped by the individual's interactions in society. A number of sociologists have studied the identities of social movement members through the lens of this theory. In this section, I use the concepts and findings of this body of research to help create an understanding of the processes involved in the development of disability pride, as well as other disability identities.

Predispositions

Putnam (2005) cites studies that indicated that people who became politically active held certain preexisting beliefs, especially the belief that their problems had a political dimension and were not merely personal. In explaining a process of attraction to other types of social movements, J. Lofland and R. Stark (1965) describe a state of "seekership," in which potential converts see their situation as problematic and undertake a search for solutions. Certainly, those who do not see their disability as problematic in any way are less likely to become involved in the disability rights movement than those with other predispositions.

H. B. Kaplan and X. Liu (2000) argue that low self-esteem is an important predisposing factor in joining a social movement. In a longitudinal study, they found that adolescents' negative attitudes about themselves were associated with social movement membership later in life. They explain this finding in the following way: "a stigmatized identity sets the individual apart from the mutually exclusive category of nonstigmatized individuals and disposes those with a spoiled identity to participate in social movements that legitimate oneself" (232–233). T. J. Owens and P. J. Aronson (2000), however, argue that *high* self-esteem predisposes a person to join a social movement. They suggest that individuals with high self-esteem who feel threatened by societal disapproval of their identity may join a social movement to validate their self-esteem. Certainly some disability rights activists, especially early movement leaders, may fit this interpretation. However, numerous accounts by movement members report that encountering the movement's social model–based ideology was a turning point that changed the way they viewed themselves and their disabilities.

Owens and Aronson (2000) also assert that perceptions of unfairness and injustice play a role in an individual's decision to join a social movement. Indeed, many disability rights activists seem to have had a strong sense of justice prior to entering the movement, and some were involved in other protest movements before they joined the disability rights movement (DRM). Many have mentioned prior personal experiences of oppression that influenced their movement involvement. A. Asch (1984, 551) points out that many disability rights activists "had been in the mainstream [from childhood] and had never questioned their right to be there." She views their activism as a response to challenges to this sense of entitlement.

These predispositions are not sufficient to explain movement membership, however. Isolated individuals with low self-esteem and/or a sense of oppression may believe that their feelings and experiences are unique. Exposure to the dominant medical model is likely to make them feel deviant or even responsible for their own situation. In order to become activists, they must experience a turning point that will change their definition of the situation.

Turning Points

A turning point often results from an encounter between a disabled person and a movement member. Prior to this encounter, the person may have accepted the medical model and a stigma-based identity. In social movements, potential members learn, often for the first time, that their concerns are shared and that these concerns are political, not personal. As one activist recalled, "It was when I found out about the disability rights movement that I began to say, 'Of course other people can see this too; it isn't just one crazy lady out there' . . . That was just the most exciting thing that happened to me" (McCarthy 2003, 218). Similarly, Cameron writes,

> I still regarded this as my own problem. . . . It is easy as a person with impairments to come to identify yourself as "the problem," when all the signals and messages you receive from outside confirm this. When, in 1992, I first came across the disabled people's movement . . . I finally felt at home. I was able, for the first time, to take on the understanding that impairment is something we have, while disability is a social construction based on the exclusion of those who have impairments. . . . I was able to work with disabled people as a disabled person in order to challenge and break down the social barriers by which we are marginalized, ostracized and excluded . . . I had "come out" as disabled. (Swain and Cameron 1999, 73)

Finally, a woman disabled from birth describes her turning point:

> [In this job] it was the first time I had had any contact with people with other disabilities and I benefited a lot by talking about my own experiences and listening to theirs. I suddenly wasn't on my own. They all seemed proud to be disabled and it was a part of them and for the first time I realized that I was who I was because of my disability and that it could be a positive thing. (Thomas 1999b, p. 53)

An experience of discrimination may also serve as a turning point. L. A. Schur (1998) cites the case of a woman who, after finding that none of the changing rooms in a department store was accessible, made the acquaintance of a disability rights activist and subsequently became involved in the movement.

Turning points take various forms, including both face-to-face and cyberspace encounters. Although some individuals are attracted to social movements by their ideologies alone, a more common path seems to include the development of a significant relationship with someone who is already a member. The most common precipitating event in religious conversion is falling in love with *a person* of a different religion, rather than with the tenets of the religion itself. Similarly, Lofland and Stark (1965) and others have reported that attraction to a religious cult typically requires the development of an emotional bond between the potential convert and a cult member.

In other types of social movements as well, a personal connection often plays an important role in conversion to the movement's ideology. As I noted earlier in this book, early disability rights movements grew out of preexisting friendships in institutions and organizations that served people with disabilities. Similarly, Schur (1998, 15) cites the case of a man who had been a "conservative type of person" prior to his spinal injury but found "a 'special energy' and camaraderie among the patients at the VA hospital" during his rehabilitation and who eventually became a disability rights activist as a result of interactions in this new friendship group. Schur also reports the case of a woman who was invited by a school friend to "'a really nice group' of 'professional people who just happened to have disabilities.'" This woman discovered that her new friends were involved in disability rights issues, and she "soon became politically active herself" (24).

Such examples illustrate the importance of opportunity structures in the careers of disability rights activists. As Schur writes, "there are no apparent prerequisites for who can become active in disability rights politics, and . . . circumstances—the types of groups, information, and opportunities that are available—may often play a large role in politicization" (1998, 26).

Identity Work

An encounter with a disability rights activist is only the beginning of the process of identity change. Subsequent interactions redefine and refine an individual's disability identity and self-concept. The concept of "identity work" was defined by D. A. Snow and L. Anderson (1987, 1348) as "the range of activities individuals engage in to create, present, and sustain personal identities that are congruent with and supportive of the self-concept." Snow and D. McAdam (2000) describe several interactional processes that result in identity change, including identity amplification, identity consolidation, identity extension, and identity transformation.

Identity amplification "involves the embellishment and strengthening of an existing identity that is congruent with a movement's collective identity but not sufficiently salient to ensure participation and activism" (Snow and McAdam 2000, 49). In the case of the DRM, a potential member might already have relatively high self-esteem as a result of positive feedback from significant others. However, the individual might not yet have disability pride. Another scenario might involve an individual who had some inclination to think of him or herself as an activist but had not acted on that inclination.

Identity consolidation refers to "the adoption of an identity that combines two prior identities that appear to be incompatible" (Snow and McAdam 2000, 50). Possibly, in the context of the DRM, a person whose previous activism was unrelated to his or her disability might reformulate an activist identity to include advocacy on behalf of his or her disability identity. In fact, a number of prominent disability rights activists were previously active in other political movements.

Identity extension involves the expansion of one's personal identity to be congruent with the collective identity of the movement. As a result, the individual comes to enact his or her role as member in all social situations, even outside formal movement-related activities. Not all movement members adopt this position, but some of the more outspoken members of the DRM may see their personal and movement identities as interchangeable.

Unlike the three previous construction processes, identity transformation involves the replacement of an old identity with a new one. The individuals quoted earlier about their turning points would fit into this category. Because of the pervasiveness of the medical model in society, this process may in fact be the most common one for members of the DRM. The literature certainly suggests a movement from shame to pride among those who move from apathy to activism.

K. J. Kiecolt (2000) states that self-concept change in social movements can take various forms. First, a person's hierarchy of identities might change through the addition of a new identity, the removal of an old one, or a change in the salience of existing identities. Thus, a person might add the identity of activist, delete the identity of victim, or more highly value an identity of disability pride. Second, the meanings of an identity might change. For example, a person who had a negative view of activism prior to joining the DRM might redefine the activist role and its associated identity in positive terms.

According to Snow and McAdam (2000), identity construction occurs through "framing processes," which include talk and collective action that shape the definition of the situation among participants. Kiecolt (2000) describes a process of "internalization" through which the self-concept changes to reflect behavior. Through interaction, participants define each other and shape individual identities in accordance with the group's collective identity. Although these authors do not mention it by name, the mechanism through which definitions are shaped is role-taking. This mechanism, discussed in Chapters 1 and 3, involves learning the language of the group in order to understand and share its meanings. Through these shared understandings, new members learn to see the world and themselves in the same way as those who already belong.

Kiecolt (2000) describes three kinds of interaction that characterize identity work in social movements:

Narrative: Participants tell stories about themselves and their experiences. These stories reinforce the identities of the tellers and enable listeners to perceive commonalities between the tellers' experiences and their own. In the case of the DRM, publications like the *Disability Rag* also serve as forums for storytelling, along with biographical accounts like John Hockenberry's *Moving Violations* and Harriet McBride Johnson's *Too Late to Die Young.* A number of writers have viewed narratives as the basis for identity construction (see, e.g., Somers, cited in Thomas 1999b, 119–120).

Rituals: These include symbolic actions such as protest songs and marches and parades that celebrate an identity such as gay pride. The disability culture movement has in recent decades included poetry, dance, theater, and other forms of expression (see, e.g., Fries 1997). Kiecolt argues that these rituals serve to reaffirm the identities of movement members.

Confrontation: The social movement literature describes the importance of in-group solidarity versus out-group opposition. By naming a common enemy, members reinforce their in-group identity. The enemy has taken a number of forms in the case of the DRM, including legislators who have not supported disability rights legislation, employers who have discriminated against people with disabilities, nondisabled people who have parked in spots designated for those with disabilities, and individuals who have committed hate crimes against the disabled, among others. "Us" and "them" discussions among members serve to sharpen and increase the salience of the "us" identity.

An additional element not mentioned by Kiecolt or Snow and McAdam is emotional attachment. As noted in Chapter 3, individuals are likely to pay more attention to definitions from significant others than to those from others who are not important to them. Typically, social movement involvement is not merely intellectual or cognitive. Self-concept change grows out of real or perceived close relationships with those who offer new definitions of oneself. In addition, as noted previously, people are generally more receptive to positive self-definitions than to negative ones, because they want to feel good about themselves.

L. Britt and D. Heise (2000) assert that people who have experienced stigma and its attendant shame tend to be predisposed toward movements that foster pride. They describe the process by which social movements transform feelings of vulnerability and fear into anger against "the system" that provokes these feelings. Anger and indignation occur as a result of the externalization of the problem. In addition, "seeing one's own feelings and actions in others generates empathic unity and a sense of alliance" (Britt and Heise 2000, 263). As a result, the "emotional capital" that accrues through movement participation enables the self to embrace feelings of solidarity and pride.

A Model of the Development of Disability Pride

In a classic text on the social psychology of social movements, H. Toch (1965, 122) asserts that movement affiliation "tends to occur when a person whose adherence to the *status quo* has been weakened encounters a plausible solution, at a point of high susceptibility." This assertion summarizes the conditions discussed in the previous section. Individuals with disabilities who have experienced stigma in their interactions in conventional society are likely to be susceptible to the appeal of a movement that redefines their discomfort as a social problem and offers a solution in the form of social change. However, as I explained in the previous section, an encounter with a movement representative is just the beginning of the "conversion" process. The individual's attachment to the movement and its principles needs to be nurtured through interactions with significant others that involve narratives, rituals, and confrontations. Figure 5.1 depicts the career path of a potential DRM member on both a cognitive and an emotional level.

Figure 5.1 The Path of Identity Change in Becoming a Disability Activist

	Predisposing Factors		Turning Point		Identity Work
Cognitive Level	Negative disability identity and/or sense of injustice	——➤ *seekership*	Encounter with new significant other	——➤	Exposure to movement ideology ——➤ *role-taking*	Redefinition of self
Emotional Level	Shame ——➤		Attachment ——➤		Solidarity, Anger ——➤	Pride

Identity Diversity

Although the association between activism and pride appears to be a strong one, activism may not be the only path to disability pride, and pride may not be the most salient identity for all activists. Asch (1984) asserts that at least some activists engage in activism mostly out of a sense of injustice that arises from neither shame nor pride in their disability. Many with lifelong disabilities tend to view themselves positively, whether or not they become involved in disability rights activism.

Also, as noted earlier, only a minority of people with disabilities become activists; yet, as the literature review in Chapter 2 indicated, many have high self-esteem. A. Hogan's (1999, 83) description of a woman named Carol, who became deaf in adulthood, illustrates a different path to positive self-esteem:

> Reeling from marginalizing encounters, she remarked: "I was becoming very much an introvert. . . . I was isolating myself from people." . . . Carol's [comments] . . . encapsulate the marginalizing process, often described using Goffman's (1963) notion of stigma and spoiled identity . . . when a person is confronted with the threat of marginalization, they may experience a sense of shame, guilt or anxiety because they recognize that they lack something or possess something considered by others to be undesirable. . . .
>
> Carol subsequently met other people who were in a similar situation. This group had developed skills and communication tactics generally found to be acceptable to hearing people, which supposedly meant that they could "pass" as hearing people. Carol's feelings about herself changed as did her social activities and networks.

This example shows that passing, or minimizing one's disability, may also lead to self-pride. Like the disability activists discussed earlier, Carol experienced a turning point when she encountered new significant others. However, her new friends were not trying to change society; consistent with a medical model, they were trying to change themselves to fit better into society. Yet the outcome for Carol was the same—a more positive identity.

Of course, passing is not an option for those with obvious disabilities that cannot be hidden, which may explain why prominent disability activists have tended to be people with significant, visible impairments. These comments on the listserv of the Society for Disability Studies (SDS) suggest an association between activism and visibility:

> I'm coming from a place of having experienced many years of non-apparent disability, and many years of apparent disability. . . . I personally started out, after the first few years, emphatically identifying "disabled." . . . 12 years later, when things got better, I felt like I was quite ready for a break from "disability identity." . . . I think that this was particularly true because living with "apparent" disability, and a very nontraditional wheelchair, had generated a lot of attention that I didn't want, so it was rather nice to leave it behind. . . . At the same time as discussing and lobbying for empowerment, some of the attitudes of the disability movement come across to me as quite disempowering, . . . and I wanted to get away from that.
>
> Then along came a slightly different version of increased mobility disability, and I'm presently solidly back in the "apparent" category. . . . After about one year, I decided it was time to really acknowledge the situation. . . . This has made for quite a quandary as far as my "disability identity." Do I go back to "identifying disabled," or rather incongruously try to maintain some distance from that identity? Obviously, since I joined [a disability organization with an activist stance], it's not entirely the latter! (SDS Listserv 2006)

Clearly, those with disabilities that are not readily apparent have more choices with regard to their identities than those who are immediately stigmatized. Moreover, choices are structured by the opportunities that are available. Many people with disabilities never encounter the DRM ideology or the social model in their everyday interactions. (See Chapter 6 for more on the relationship between identities and opportunities and a typology that includes the entire range of disability orientations.)

The model of disability identity development presented in this chapter could be used to explain identities other than activism-based pride as well. As self and identity theories suggest, all identities result from interaction in society. As individuals move through the life course, they are likely to encounter new significant others whose views differ from those they have known in the past. Those with more economic and social resources are especially likely to have the opportunity to experience turning points that might result in self-concept change. In general, everyone seeks to have a positive self-image. As a result, turning points that produce positive definitions of the self are most likely to have an impact on the individual.

Clearly, the career path of individuals born with a disability will not be the same as that of individuals who acquire a disability later in life. (See Chapter 8 for more about the importance of the timing of disability onset.) Thomas (1999a, 53) notes that acquired disability is likely to be associated with an unwelcome change in self-concept, as illustrated by this quote from a woman with multiple sclerosis: "I was reluctant to define myself as disabled, carrying as I did all of the prejudices I had somehow adopted in my able-bodied days." This woman goes on to describe the positive change in her self-concept that resulted from her discovery of the DRM.

The growth of disability culture and the DRM in recent years continues to provide an increasing number of opportunities for people with disabilities to encounter the social model and the identity of disability pride. Perhaps, then, this identity will be assumed by an increasing number of individuals in the years ahead. However, as I suggest in Chapters 6 and 7, other identities continue to characterize many, and probably most, people with disabilities in today's society.

Conclusion

The disability rights movement has increased opportunities for disabled people to be exposed to more positive definitions of themselves and their disabilities and has come to be associated with the identity of disability pride. However, the career paths of people with disabilities appear to be quite variable. Those who become activists appear to follow a career path that is similar to those of members of other social movements. Social psychological theory suggests that potential members have predispositions, such as a strong sense of justice, along with personal feelings of injustice. The membership process generally begins with an encounter with a movement member and is followed by the development of significant relationships within the movement. New members come to adopt the movement's ideology through various forms of interaction and eventually come to see themselves differently.

6

The Diversity of
Disability Orientations

In this chapter, I shift focus slightly from the concept of disability identity to that of disability orientation. As explained in Chapter 1, disability orientation is broader than disability identity and includes the related variables of identity, model, and role. The polar types of each of these variables are as follows:

- Identity: pride and shame.
- Model: social model and medical model.
- Role: activism and passivity.

Typically, pride has been associated with the social model and activism, and shame has been associated with the medical model and passivity. However, other combinations are possible. I explore the interrelationships among these variables in this chapter. The typology that emerges, like many typologies in sociology, proposes ideal types that only approximate actual orientations. These types are useful in understanding the diversity of orientations that exist among people with disabilities, but most people exhibit only aspects of these orientations and approach the ideal types to a greater or lesser degree.

As I noted in previous chapters, in the past, most orientations toward disability were based on a medical model, and people with disabilities were commonly categorized on the basis of whether or not they had "accepted" their limitations and adapted to them. More recently, a social model, which shifts the focus from the individual to the larger society, has become popular. However, not all people with

disabilities share a common perspective. Because research and practice need to address diverse segments of this population, the development of models that reflect the entire range of disability orientations
is important. I draw both from research about people with disabilities
and from writings by people with disabilities in order to develop a
model of disability orientations in the contemporary population of
people with disabilities.

Why is a typology of orientations needed? Certainly, developers
of typologies need to be cautious about pigeonholing people, which
tends to promote stereotyping and a lack of attention to individual
differences. However, ideal types have both theoretical and practical
value. From a theoretical standpoint, the existence of categories provides a basis for delineating empirical possibilities and a starting
point for research into the correlates, antecedents, and effects of various categorical realities. For example, if one type includes individuals who internalize societal stigma toward disability and another includes those who reject such negative views, studying those who
typify these positions would shed light on the personal characteristics
and social interactions that serve as filters of social norms. Previous
research on race, for example, showed that most African Americans
did not have low self-esteem, even though the norms of the larger society favored whiteness. As M. Rosenberg and R. G. Simmons
(1971) and others have shown, African Americans tend to interact
with race-based reference groups that reject the norms of the white
majority. As I noted in earlier chapters, similar processes seem to op-
erate in the case of other stigmatized groups, such as people with disabilities.

Applications of knowledge based on research using a typology of
disability orientations would be valuable as well. If research indicated, for example, that certain categories of individuals with disabilities were more likely to have high self-esteem or to participate in desired social activities, practitioners and policymakers might engage
in activities to assist individuals in the acquisition of resources that
enabled them to become part of those categories. If disability activism were the goal, and certain types were shown to be associated
with activism, movement leaders might benefit from this information, because it would assist them in locating potential recruits for
the disability rights movement. As Putnam writes (2005, 188),
"Knowing why some people experiencing disability support and become involved in disability rights issues and others do not is critical
to understanding disability politics."

A Typology Based on the Normalization Model

About thirty years ago (Darling 1979), I developed a typology of adaptations among parents of children with disabilities. Interviews with families had suggested four ideal types, as shown in Table 6.1. These types were based on opportunity structure theory (Cloward and Ohlin 1960). This theory is derived, in turn, from anomie theory (Merton 1949), which begins with the premise that most people in society desire the same goals. In the case of people with disabilities (or their parents), those goals seemed to include "normalization," or a lifestyle that was similar to that of people who did not have disabilities. (This use of the term *normalization* is a little broader than its common usage in the intellectual disability literature.) For families with children, such a lifestyle included access to good medical care, appropriate educational placement, employment for one or both parents, adequate financial resources, leisure time, relationships with friends and relatives, access to public places, and recreational opportunities.

Because of a variety of physical, social, and cultural barriers, not all families of children with disabilities were able to achieve normalization. Among the most common barriers were physicians who preferred not to treat these children, inadequate child care arrangements, and the failure of schools to provide opportunities for inclusion in regular classrooms. Some families, however, were able to overcome these barriers with the help of supportive friends and relatives, sympathetic physicians and employers, and accommodating school districts, among other opportunities. Even families who had children with severe impairments achieved normalization with adequate support.

Table 6.1 Modes of Adaptation Among Parents of Children with Disabilities

	Type of Integration	
Mode of Adaptation	Normal Society	Alternative Subculture (disability as a "career")
Normalization	+	−
Crusadership	−	+
Altruism	+	+
Resignation	−	−

Notes: + indicates integration achieved; − indicates integration withdrawn or not achieved.

Still, for many families, normalization was an elusive goal. These families engaged in "crusadership" in order to attain a normalized lifestyle, which included activities such as lobbying school officials, changing doctors, and creating new programs. These parents typically worked with other parents to achieve their goals, and many belonged to organized advocacy groups. These groups, in turn, were part of a larger disability subculture, consisting of various local, state, and national organizations, as well as the literature that these organizations produced. Crusadership was more common in middle- and upper-class families, although some working-class families also adopted this orientation. Most parents who adopted a crusadership mode maintained that adaptation only until their families were able to achieve some degree of normalization. At that point, they commonly decreased their association with other families of children with disabilities and with the disability subculture in general.

However, a few crusaders continued to have an activist orientation, even after their own families had achieved normalization. These "altruists" continued to work for social change for other people's children. In some cases, altruists also reaped personal rewards from their involvement as leaders of disability organizations.

Finally, some families had neither access to opportunities for normalization nor access to the disability subculture. These families included those living in isolated, rural areas, those who did not speak English, and those too overwhelmed by problems such as poverty to focus on their children's disabilities, along with some other groups. This "resignation" adaptation generally characterized families in the least powerful segments of society.

With the exception of the altruists, none of these parents chose to identify with the disability subculture when opportunities for identification with "normal" society were available. In many cases, the desire to avoid stigma was a key motivating factor in the rejection of a disability identity. As noted in Chapter 2 and elsewhere, people with obvious disabilities have occupied a devalued or discredited status in society. As a result, people with disabilities have historically tried to pass as "normal." In the case of parents of children with disabilities, M. Voysey (1975), A. Birenbaum (1970), and others have identified strategies used to maintain a "normal-appearing round of life."

Although this typology was based on research with parents of children with disabilities, a considerable amount of evidence suggests that it also could have been applied to adults with disabilities at the time. Normalization appears to have been the most common ori-

entation among adults as well. For example, autobiographical accounts by A. Potok (1980) and others suggest an ideology of normalization, in which the authors describe successful strategies for fitting
in to "normal" society or even passing as normal. Richardson (1972,
530) quotes a young woman with cerebral palsy: "I didn't want to
know from handicapped people—they weren't me. . . . When I graduated from special school, I said, 'Thank God, no more handicapped
people.'"

Other orientations were also represented among adults. Crusadership with a goal of normalization could be found in the newsletters of disability organizations such as United Cerebral Palsy or the
Spina Bifida Association of America, which described activities designed to improve access to jobs, housing, medical care, and other
areas of life. The resignation adaptation was evident in media stories
about Elizabeth Bouvia and other adults with disabilities who wanted
to choose death over life with disability. Thus, the model seems to
describe the orientations of both adults with disabilities and parents
of children with disabilities, at least during the 1970s and 1980s.

A similar model, proposed by J. E. Nash and A. Nash (1981), relates specifically to adaptations to deafness. This model suggests that
normalization involves reliance on lipreading and speech production.
Acculturation involves the acquisition of American Sign Language
and immersion in Deaf culture. *Membership* involves immersion in
the deaf community as a way of neutralizing stigma. *Advocating* involves the complete rejection of the stigmatizing views of "normal"
society. *Passing* involves pretending to hear in an attempt to achieve
normalization. Finally, *retreating* involves failed attempts at normalization coupled with a rejection of the deaf community. The inclusion
of categories involving positive association with the deaf community
predates similar developments among people with other disabilities.
These developments are reflected in the model presented below.

Is Anomie Theory Still Relevant?

Since the publication of my work on families, the identity of at least
some individuals with disabilities has changed, and a stigma-based
identity model has been replaced by disability pride. As I have explained earlier in this book, proponents of the newer model reject the
norms of the larger society that label disabilities as failings and persons with disabilities as morally inferior to "normals." As noted in

Chapter 5, J. Swain and S. French (2000) describe an "affirmation model," which views disability as part of a positive social identity and rejects older models that view disabilities as personal tragedies. They argue that disability is increasingly being recognized as a normal form of human diversity rather than as a condition that needs to be changed or eliminated. People with disabilities who adopt this view have been characterized as "proud, angry, and strong."

The affirmation model clearly rejects the notion, based in anomie theory, that everyone in society accepts the dominant cultural norms with regard to abilities and appearances. If, in fact, this model is rapidly replacing older views, the normalization-based typology described above may be obsolete. Even so, the actual identities of people with disabilities today remain an empirical question. Although many disability activists clearly adhere to the newer model, large numbers of individuals with disabilities who are not part of recent social movements may continue to accept the older views and regard themselves as victims of personal misfortune.

Toward a New Typology

A typology of current disability orientations needs to include both the normalization and affirmation models, along with any other orientations that were found to exist. In order to develop such a typology, I reviewed a considerable amount of recent literature about and by people with disabilities and parents of children with disabilities. This literature included numerous autobiographical accounts (e.g., Kisor 1990; Kuusisto 1998; Mairs 1996), media accounts for both lay and professional audiences, writings by movement activists, and published studies of various disabled populations by social scientists and other academic researchers. This literature review suggested that orientations to disability do indeed reflect differential access to opportunities to achieve either normalization or the alternative—affirmative definitions promoted through disability culture and disability rights movements—or both.

Table 6.2 depicts the typology suggested by my literature review, with the types renamed to reflect more current language. I based this table on my finding that two primary orientations to disability appear to exist. The cultural majority orientation includes acceptance of and/or access to generally accepted norms about appearance and ability based on cultural values of attractiveness and achievement. The

Table 6.2 A Typology of Disability Orientations

	Norms/Goals of Cultural Majority		Norms/Goals of Disability Subculture	
	Access	Acceptance	Access	Acceptance
Typicality	+	+	+/–	–
Personal activism	–	+	+	–
Affirmative activism	+/–	–	+	+
Situational identification	+	+	+	+
Resignation	–	+	–	–
Apathy	+/–	–	+/–	–
Isolated affirmative activism	–	–	–	+

Notes: + indicates has access or accepts; – indicates does not have access or does not accept; +/– indicates may or may not have access.

minority, or subcultural, orientation involves acceptance of and/or access to alternative norms about appearance and ability, based on a value of diversity. Access and acceptance do not necessarily coexist in the same individual. In some cases, individuals may have access to opportunities for success in the societal mainstream but may choose to reject mainstream norms in favor of identification with the minority. Conversely, individuals who do not have opportunities for inclusion in mainstream society may identify with the majority nonetheless. In other cases, individuals may have access to the minority subculture but may not choose to identify with it or may accept its norms even though they are isolated from it. Each of the types will be described in greater detail below, along with illustrative examples from my literature review.

Typicality (formerly Normalization)

Individuals who adopt this orientation are those who accept the norms of the larger society with regard to appearance and/or ability and who manage to achieve lifestyles that are similar to those of individuals of their social status who do not have disabilities. Those with disabilities that are not highly visible may even choose to pass as "normal." Typically, these individuals have supportive families and employers and have sufficient financial resources to purchase other supports that may be needed, such as accessible housing. They are likely to welcome rehabilitation efforts by professionals, as well as technological advances such as cochlear implants that allow them to function more "normally." Conversely, they may reject stigma symbols, such as white canes or orthopedic appliances. Most of their social interactions center around individuals without disabilities. As one woman writes, "Long ago I recognised that being close to other disabled people, especially those with similar impairments, was too like looking in a mirror" (Thomas 1999b, 51). A good example of this orientation is Henry Kisor (1990), a deaf journalist working for a major newspaper who functions well orally, is married to a hearing person, and whose social life takes place almost exclusively within the hearing world.

In some cases, the desire for typicality is so strong that an individual may choose to believe that he or she is functioning "normally," even without necessary supports. S. Kuusisto (1998) describes how he moved in "normal" social circles for many years, even though his vision was extremely limited, and J. Hockenberry (1995) discusses his insistence on working in inaccessible places even though he relied on a wheelchair for mobility. Similarly, N. Mairs (1996, 100–101) quotes her mother-in-law, a resident of a retirement community in Arizona, as saying, "You know, over fifty percent of the people who live here now use wheelchairs or walkers or oxygen tanks. It's *so* depressing," even though she has significant disabilities herself. I have observed the same phenomenon in the retirement community in California where my mother lives. As M. Priestley and P. Rabiee (2002, 605) suggest, "the emphasis on maintaining positive old age identities and generational networks of support [may require] a purposeful distancing from discourses of disability."

L. A. Schur (1998, 12–13) offers an example of a woman who tries to maintain role distance from other people with disabilities:

> I don't go to all of those special meetings with a bunch of other people sitting in wheelchairs 'cause to me that's too depressing. . . . I'm lucky enough that I have my friends and my family so it helps me keep my mind off of this stupid wheelchair. . . . So by staying away from other people in wheelchairs it kind of . . . makes me feel like I'm having a normal day.

Not all individuals who define themselves in normative terms accept the stigmatized image of disability that typically accompanies this perspective. N. Watson (2002, 521) presents data from a number of disabled respondents who neither deny their disability nor view it with pride. For these individuals, their disability is not the most salient part of their identity; rather, they tend to see themselves as "normal" people who "happen to have" a disability: "Being disabled, for many of these informants, is not about celebrating difference or diversity, pride in their identity is not formed through the individuals labeling themselves as different, as disabled, but it is about defining disability in their own terms, under their own terms of reference." Similarly, Asch (2004, 29) writes of her disability, "I do not find this facet of my life and identity inherently interesting." Although she does not celebrate her disability identity, neither does she view it negatively. For her, disability is but one aspect of a self-concept that includes many other, often more salient, identities.

"Feeling normal" is also situationally variable. M. J. Deegan (2010) explains that disability consciousness tends to arise in partic-ular social situations such as medical settings or encounters with physical barriers. She argues that "feeling normal" is not a denial of disability. Rather, like Watson, she suggests that disability may not be an especially salient identity in everyday life. Similarly, S. F. Gilson and E. DePoy (2004, 20) quote a respondent as saying, "I deal with my disability when it is shoved in my face like when I have to do something in a practical way or I have to fill out some papers and then I get on with being just a human being."

This version of typicality may not include an identity as strong as disability pride, yet shame is rejected as well. As one woman re-marked in response to a question about whether she would want a cure for her disability if one were available, "Who am I if I'm not a disabled person? . . . This is part of my identity. . . . I can't sacrifice who I am to become the one you want me to be" (Disability Research Discussion List 2004).

The typicality orientation, then, may or may not include accept-ance of societal stigma. In the next chapter, I explore the nature of this orientation further using empirical evidence. Because of the per-vasiveness of the majority culture and its norms, a typicality orienta-tion, with or without the internalization of stigma, may be the most common one among disabled people of all ages in the Western world today.

Personal Activism (formerly Crusadership)

As described in my earlier work (Darling 1979), personal activists, or crusaders, are those who accept the norms of the cultural majority but who do not have access to a typical lifestyle. Consequently, they become involved in the disability subculture in an attempt to achieve typicality. Their activities may include advocacy, as well as involvement in larger social movements in order to create typicality-promoting social change. For example, during the 1970s in the United States, parents of children with spina bifida engaged in court battles to force school personnel to perform clean intermittent catheterization to enable their children to receive regular public education. Typically, when their activism was successful, these individuals would adopt a typicality orientation.

A more recent example of a personal activism orientation would be the late actor Christopher Reeve. After his paralysis in an equestrian accident, Reeve campaigned for research into a cure for spinal injuries. Although his celebrity afforded him access to a wealth of resources, the visibility and extent of his disability prevented him from achieving the typicality he desired. Consequently, he espoused a medical model, rather than simply affirming his new identity as a person with a disability.

The "lone wolves" described by Schur (1998) seem to be a subgroup of the personal activism type. These individuals do not join disability organizations, but they work nonetheless to raise public awareness, change laws, or reform the rehabilitation system in order to regain control over their lives.

Affirmative Activism

Like personal activists, affirmative activists identify with the disability subculture in order to achieve their goals. However, unlike personal activists, their identification is not temporary. The goal for these individuals is not typicality. Although they may seek access to the right to participate fully in society, they continue to view their disability as their primary identity and to view it in positive terms. As I noted in Chapter 5, some writers have referred to this orientation in terms of "coming out" as a person with a disability (see, e.g., Gill 1997).

Disability pride seems to include two aspects: self-esteem and separation. M. Russell (1994, 13) likens disability pride to the black pride that arose from the US civil rights movement: "like Malcolm [X], disabled people must learn to celebrate our own bodies and respect who we are." The second aspect involves the rejection of assimilation or the notion of a melting pot. C. J. Gill (1994, 49) argues that ability and disability do not exist on a continuum and that people who are negatively labeled by society occupy a separate and distinct social status. People who do not share this experience of oppression cannot identify as disabled. She goes on to say, "politically and psychologically our power will come from celebrating who we are as a distinct people." Many leaders of the disability rights movement seem to share this view, and disability movements and the rise of disability culture clearly have contributed toward viewing disability in a positive light.

Situational Identification

Some people are chameleons. They seem to be able to maintain multiple identities or to adopt whatever identity seems appropriate or expedient at any given time. In some cases, these identity shifts simply reflect ambivalence, or the inability or unwillingness to choose between competing norms. Thus, some disabled individuals who have access to full inclusion in society may choose typicality when interacting with individuals without disabilities but may reject typicality norms when interacting with their disabled peers.

This orientation is more complex than the "altruism" adaptation I described in my earlier work. Altruists were parents who continued to identify with the disability subculture even after their own children had achieved typicality, ostensibly to fight for other children who were not as fortunate as their own. They were crusaders who continued their personal activism rather than choosing the easier alternative of typicality.

True situational identifiers would, at least at times, adopt the norms of affirmation, especially if they desire acceptance within the disability community. However, affirmative activists may not accept such individuals into the fold (Gill 1994). Because of the difficulties inherent in trying to live in two worlds, situational identifiers may eventually choose one identity or the other.

Some situational identifiers may simply be engaging in self-presentation (see Chapter 3 for a further discussion of this concept) in order to obtain some desired right or privilege. In his classic description of the "sick role," T. Parsons (1951) argues that those who are sick are entitled to certain benefits or privileges, such as not having to report for work. Similarly, people with disabilities have been awarded monetary and other benefits as a result of legislation such as workers' compensation laws. More recently, legislation such as the Americans with Disabilities Act has granted certain rights to this population, including the requirement that employers accommodate their disability. Such benefits and rights provide an incentive for some individuals to claim disability, even when it is not actually part of their identity. In fact, as I show in Chapter 7, some individuals who have been identified as disabled choose to agree with the statement, "I don't think of myself as a disabled person." Thus, one variant of situational identification may be pragmatic identification, which may, in fact, not be true identification at all.

Resignation

Some individuals who desire, but are unable to achieve, typicality do not have access to the disability subculture either. They may be illiterate or living in poverty or in isolated rural areas without access to a computer. Such individuals are more likely to be exposed to the norms of the majority culture than to those of the disability subculture because of the dominance of the majority view in the media and in society in general. Thus, they do not have the resources to achieve typicality but also lack opportunities to learn about affirmation. This population is perhaps the least studied group of people with disabilities and the least likely to be empowered to speak for itself.

As I reported in Chapter 4, P. Devlieger and G. Albrecht (2000, 58) suggest that the inner-city individuals they interviewed were more focused on issues of poverty and racism than they were on their disabilities: "In a way, one could say that in the inner-city cultural context, there is no time to deal with a disability." In some ways, their respondents had more of a typicality than a resignation orientation because, like the people in the study by Watson described earlier, they did not define themselves primarily in terms of their disabilities. However, unlike Watson's respondents, they did seem to accept society's negative definition of disability, based on a medical model.

Apathy

To include all logical possibilities in the typology, one would need to acknowledge that some individuals might simply be apathetic or completely uninformed. This category might include people with significant mental illness or intellectual disability. Such individuals might be truly unaware of the norms of either the majority culture or the disability subculture. In a review of studies of social identity in people with intellectual disabilities, for example, Beart and colleagues (2005) found that some members of this population appeared to be unaware of the label that had been attached to them, but some did experience stigma on an emotional level and did not like being "different." This lack of awareness was unrelated to their access to opportunities for typicality.

Isolated Affirmative Activism

Finally, some individuals who do not have access to the disability subculture may, on their own, arrive at an orientation of affirmative activism. Sociological knowledge about the processes of socialization suggests that such an outcome is highly unlikely. However, the possibility of innovation based on ideas derived from other social movements or related social situations cannot be excluded. The founders of the disability rights movement exemplify this type. Early leaders of the movement in the United States, such as Ed Roberts, advocated affirmative activism long before it was a common disability identity. Today, isolated affirmative activists would be likely to join the disability subculture upon learning of its existence.

Empirical Evidence

Although no study has determined the percentage of the disabled population that would fit into each of the types described above, some evidence suggests that the affirmation categories may represent a larger share of the population today than they did in the past. As I noted in Chapter 5, a national survey conducted in the United States in 2000 (National Organization on Disability 2000) found that among the disabled population as a whole, 47 percent shared a sense of common identity with other people with disabilities. This percentage had increased by seven points from a similar survey conducted in 1986. However, people who identify with other people with disabilities do not necessarily accept the norms and goals of the disability subculture or the disability rights movement. Many of these individuals may simply see themselves as part of a group of fellow sufferers who are not able to achieve typicality.

In Chapter 7, I report the findings of an empirical study that supported the existence of the typology described above. However, the study did not use a representative sample of the population of people with disabilities, and further research is needed to ascertain the patterns and trends in the orientations of individuals with disabilities in today's society.

Careers: Identity Change over Time

The typology described above can be applied to the orientation of a given individual at any point in time. However, identities are not static and are likely to change over time. Symbolic interaction theory suggests that our identities and self-concepts are products of our interactions in society (see Chapter 3). Consequently, we continually readjust our identities to reflect new self-definitions received from others.

An example of identity change is the case of Larry James McAfee, a man with significant disabilities who initially represents the resignation mode (Shapiro 1994). McAfee had no exposure to the disability subculture and was unaware of options for independent living. As a result, he was depressed and said that he wanted to die. When his situation received media attention, disability activists became involved in his case and helped him advocate for an improved living situation. Interaction with these activists made him aware of resources he never knew existed and changed his prior definition of his situation as "hopeless." Consequently, he moved from a position of resignation to one of personal activism.

J. Tollifson provides another example of identity change, this time from resignation to affirmative activism. In "Imperfection Is a Beautiful Thing" (quoted in Chapter 3), she writes about using drugs and alcohol prior to joining a group of disabled women on the advice of her therapist. As a result, she "began to realize that my supposedly private hell was a social phenomenon" (Tollifson 1997, 111). Her encounters with the therapist and the group of disabled women served as turning points that changed the direction of her life.

Conceivably, turning points could produce other kinds of identity and orientation change. For example, a person experiencing stigma might move to a new community where he or she was welcomed and accepted by nondisabled associates, resulting in a shift from resignation to typicality. (See Chapter 5 for other examples of turning points.)

The movement from one identity to another over time constitutes a "career" (Becker 1963). Typically, such movement results in increasing commitment to a self-concept and the role associated with it. However, as noted earlier in this book, careers can change direction at turning points (Strauss 1962), when individuals enter new interaction situations and encounter new definitions. Personal activism typically becomes transformed into typicality after one or more turning points during which new opportunities become available. For example, an individual with a disability who is hired for his first job may choose to disassociate himself from the disability community and to develop new relationships with his nondisabled coworkers. Some individuals who have adopted a typicality or personal activism orientation, however, may move to an affirmative activism orientation after meeting a disability activist or encountering the literature of the disability rights movement.

Using a psychological model of identity development based in personality theory, Carol Gill suggests a career path resulting in affirmative activism (see Chapter 5 for an explanation of her theory). She argues that the first step in the path toward personality integration for people with disabilities is "coming to feel we belong," or integrating into society. At this stage, individuals begin to reject the notion that they are to blame for their differences from the societal norm. During the second stage, "coming home," individuals begin to integrate with a disability community they may have rejected in the past. In the third stage, "coming together," individuals accept their disability and see themselves as whole. Finally, the last step is a "coming out" process." It "is often the last step toward disability identity in a path that begins with a desire to find a place in society, continues with a discovery of one's place in a community of peers, and builds to an appreciation and acceptance of one's whole self complete with disability" (Gill 1997, 45). As a psychologist, Gill is particularly concerned with the development of positive identities. Consequently, she does not dwell on the sociological conditions that may enable movement from one stage to another. Moreover, because she sees coming out as the desired outcome, she does not consider career paths that are likely to result in other outcomes, such as successful typicality. She may be correct in arguing that coming out (or affirmation) is the only outcome that would produce high self-esteem, but the self-esteem of people with various identities is an empirical question. Some support for Gill's position can be found in other studies. For example, Schur (1998, 21) found that the highly politically active respondents in her study of people with physical disabilities reported "greater perceived control over their lives and higher satisfaction with daily life than the rest of the sample." However, perhaps individuals who achieve typicality and perceive themselves as having "overcome" their disabilities are able to maintain a high level of self-esteem as well, as a result of their "success." In a recent study (Nario-Redmond et al. 2011), *both* working to overcome one's disability and working for social change were found to be associated with a positive sense of self.

Self-Presentation

As symbolic interaction theory suggests, self-concepts are the conscious manifestations of what individuals believe to be "true" about themselves. However, as noted earlier, discrepancies sometimes exist between a person's self-concept and the way he or she chooses to enact that self, or play a role. E. Goffman (1958) describes the process of "presentation of self" as a form of impression management in which people engage in an attempt to convince others that they are certain "kinds" of people. For example, a person with a typicality orientation might engage in passing in order to convince a new acquaintance or employer that he or she does not have a significant disability.

The advent of electronic communication has simplified the process of self-presentation because visible attributes can be readily hidden. In a study of online communication among people with disabilities, one respondent said, "Online you can choose not to even bring it [the disability] up" (Bowker and Tuffin 2002, 333). Another said, "Enjoy the fact that 'on-line' you can be whatever you want to be . . . your disability need not be an issue. People will treat you as an equal" (335). Still another added, "Being online enables me to enjoy the world the way others do" (338). The Internet enables even those with significant, visible impairments to "play at" typicality. However, the effect of this charade on "true" identity and self-concept is unknown.

Although some instances of self-presentation involve denying or hiding one's disability, other instances involve claiming a disability that one does not truly embrace. Examples provided earlier in this chapter showed that some individuals may choose to identify as disabled in order to receive financial or other benefits. Thus, enacted identity may or may not be synonymous with true identity. Because all behavior is performance, disentangling actual from enacted identity is an ongoing challenge for researchers attempting to measure disability identity and orientation.

From Theory to Research

The model proposed above is based on a sociological perspective, in that it focuses on social opportunities and social interaction as the sources of individual identities. In such a model, the coping or adaptive abilities of individuals are seen as the products of their opportunity structures and the interactions that occur within those structures, rather than on their internal, psychological differences. By combining structural theory about access to opportunities and symbolic interactionist theory about the processes through which individuals internalize the definitions present in differing opportunity structures, the model offers a sociological basis for understanding changing disability identities and orientations.

Affirmation literature has dominated the field of disability studies since the mid-1980s. The proponents of the affirmative activism orientation tend to be well educated and very adept at communicating their message. Much of this literature presents a view of a world in which a social (or affirmation) model is replacing the older medical (or individual) model. Such a view, suggesting an in-group and an out-group, is not uncharacteristic of social movements in general, and serves a valuable purpose in promoting the rights of people with disabilities. However, sociologists need to understand all segments of the disabled population. Whether the identities of most people with disabilities have changed since the advent of the disability rights movement is an empirical question.

The typology I presented in this chapter is intended as a framework for guiding future research in the disability field, which must be both quantitative and qualitative. Large-scale surveys are needed to determine the proportion of people in the population who adhere to each of the orientations described above. Cross-cultural studies comparing the populations in different societies also would be interesting, as would the correlates of identification with each type. For example, the nature and visibility of an impairment, as well as the time of its acquisition (present at birth or acquired later in life) might be important variables in disability identity. Some evidence suggests that those with more severe impairments (National Organization on Disability 2000) and those with congenital impairments are more likely to identify with the disability community. As one individual has written, "What have I lost? I was born with . . . my impairment. . . . I . . . am very happy with who I am" (Higgins 2002). This writer goes on to suggest that those who acquire their impairments later in life might be more likely to experience a sense of loss and to identify with the medical model, and this suggestion is supported by research that I present in Chapters 7 and 8.

Another, largely unexplored, area involves the changing orientations of parents of children with disabilities. The disability rights movement has been composed primarily of adults with disabilities, and interaction between the parent movement (Darling 1988) and the disability rights movement has often been limited and even antagonistic at times (Darling 1993). One source of that antagonism has been the parents' emphasis on typicality rather than affirmation. Nondisabled parents of individuals with disabilities often have difficulty identifying with the concept of disability pride because their own identities are so bound up with their interactions in "normal" society:

> I remember my son's first wheelchair. For nearly five years, I squished him into strollers and heaved his heavy body from the stroller to the car seat, and we managed. I delayed that first wheelchair at any cost, because it meant the end of my dream that he would some day walk. . . . I had deprived him of his independence for so long, due to society's definitions of normalcy. (Avery 1999, 122)

Although some parents have been actively involved in the disability rights movement and have adopted an orientation of affirmative activism, the majority of parents may still identify with the typicality, personal activism, and resignation types. Empirical research is needed to determine the percentages of parents in each group and to compare parents with disabled adults in terms of their differing identifications.

In addition, further qualitative research would help to refine the categories proposed by this typology. Another possible research direction might involve an investigation of the connections between various disability identities and roles and current formulations of identity theory. J. Swain and C. Cameron (1999, 76) use this theory to explain the phenomenon of coming out as disabled: "Coming out, then, for disabled people, is a process of redefinition of one's personal identity through rejecting the tyranny of the *normate*, positive recognition of impairment and embracing disability as a valid social identity."

As I explained in Chapter 1, S. Stryker and colleagues argue that an individual's commitment to a role involves a process in which one identity becomes more salient than others. This process, in turn, involves interaction in social groups. Stryker and colleagues suggest that commitment to a social movement becomes more likely when an individual's entire network of social relationships reinforces relationships within the movement. Thus, identification with a movement tends to occur when all one's significant others support that identification. As I noted in Chapter 5, H. B. Kaplan and X. Liu (2000) and L. Britt and D. Heise (2000) argue that individuals with stigmatized identities are especially likely to join social movements that enhance their self-esteem. These writers would explain the affirmative activism orientation as an opportunity to convert shame into pride.

The process by which any particular disability identity becomes salient would be an important subject for qualitative research. In particular, future research about disability careers could help explain why some individuals with access to opportunities for typicality choose to identify with the minority, disability subculture. Such research would help us move beyond anomie theory in understanding the choices that people make.

Late modern and postmodern identity theory (see, e.g., A. Giddens 1991) suggests that identities include socially constructed narratives that derive from experience and change in response to situational requirements. In her discussion of gender and identity, J. Butler (1990) uses the concept of *performativity* to suggest that gender is enacted rather than inherent in an individual. Performativity also would be useful in explaining situational identification and self-presentation as discussed in this chapter. Further research is needed to determine to what degree other types of identification are performative as well. Moreover, as these theories suggest, individual identities are related to macrolevel structures and processes. Changes in disability orientations over time may reflect transformations in the significance of human capital resulting from technological and cultural change. Social movements may play a mediating role between macrolevel needs and expectations and the roles that individuals are encouraged to play, as well as the identities that accompany those roles. Further research in this area would help to explain changes in disability orientations over time.

This model, then, suggests a research agenda based on a synthesis of identity theory and anomie theory. Such an agenda would shed light on the range of identities of people with disabilities and their parents in a world that offers a variety of identity choices and opportunities. In addition, it would help us understand how people move along different career paths in their commitments to various self-concepts and roles. The purpose of such research would not be to pigeonhole people with disabilities but to help researchers and practitioners understand the social forces that shape choices and orientations and, ultimately, the quality of life of various sectors of the disabled population. Although few individuals are likely to conform completely to all aspects of the ideal types described in this chapter, the literature suggests that many probably tend toward one type or another. The typology can increase our understanding of these tendencies.

The field of disability studies today includes a mix of empirical research and ideological writings. Few studies have attempted to link these strands of work. As a result, although the ideological literature continues to expand, we know very little about the actual identities and roles of different segments of the disabled population or about how those identities and roles develop. Studies that describe the disability experience as it exists for large numbers of people in the world today are essential if we are to have a true sociology of disability.

In the next chapter I describe a study based on the operationalization of the typology suggested above. Although not based on a representative sample of the population of people with disabilities, the study provides support for the typology presented in this chapter and for the existence of a diversity of orientations toward disability in today's society.

Note

This chapter is a revised version of my article, "Toward a Model of Changing Disability Identities: A Proposed Typology and Research Agenda," *Disability and Society* 18 (2003): 881–896.

7

Measuring Disability Identity and Orientation

In the last chapter I proposed a typology of orientations toward disability based on opportunity structure theory in sociology. In order to determine whether this theoretical, literature-based typology could be tested empirically, D. A. Heckert and I (Darling and Heckert 2010a) conducted an exploratory study involving two convenience samples of people with disabilities. The results of this study supported the typology described in Chapter 6 and suggested directions for future research. In this chapter I describe the study and its findings.

As noted in earlier chapters, most research on disability identity has not been based on empirical studies of random samples of people with disabilities. Moreover, with the exception of a few studies based on samples of disability activists (See, e.g., Gill 1997; Hahn and Belt 2004), researchers have not attempted to operationalize the concept of disability identity. In order to have practical applications, a theoretical typology of identities and orientations, such as the one presented in Chapter 6, needs to be operationalized. As Putnam (2005, 204) argues,

> Despite the inherent intellectual and scientific challenges of developing, testing, and validating a disability identity measure, the venture seems important. . . . Only by empirical investigation will knowledge about disability identity move forward. We know that disability identity has been important to collective action, but we have not been able to describe or quantify it in a way that guides our intellectual understanding of disability.

The instrument to be described in this chapter makes a major contribution to addressing the methodological challenge of operationalizing the concept of disability orientation and the related concept of disability identity. Such an instrument would be valuable in further quantitative research that determined the actual prevalence of various orientations among people with disabilities in the United States today, as well as the correlates of these orientations. It could also be used in selecting subjects for qualitative research that examined the antecedents and consequences of different orientations. Finally, it might be useful to practitioners in determining appropriate intervention strategies for various individuals who use their services.

The Study

In order to begin the process of subjecting this literature-based typology to empirical testing, during the mid-2000s Heckert and I conducted an exploratory study with both qualitative and quantitative components. We wished to learn whether the proposed typology reflected actual orientations toward disability and to determine whether these types could be measured. The methods and findings are discussed below.

Methods

Qualitative component. The first phase of the research consisted of a qualitative study involving in-depth interviews with a convenience sample of ten individuals, secured through contacts with disability organizations. All ten lived in small cities or rural areas. I conducted these interviews over a period of three months, and each interview lasted about two hours. The respondents were all middle-aged or older adults. Some had lifelong disabilities, whereas others had acquired their disabilities more recently.

The interview schedule consisted of questions relating to

• Disability identity (e.g., "Is your disability an important part of who you are as a person?").
• Social/medical model (e.g., "Do you ever wish that someone would find a cure for your disability?").
• Activism (e.g., "Are you familiar with the disability rights

movement?" "Have you ever engaged in any activities to fight for your rights as a person with a disability?").

• Access to both mainstream and disability-related activities (e.g., "Have you ever been employed?" "About how often do you get together with friends or family?" "Do you have access to the Internet?" "Do you belong to any disability-related organizations?").

• Other disability-related areas suggested by the respondent.

Because an analysis of the data from this phase of the research supported the literature-based hypothesis that a variety of orientations toward disability exist, we proceeded with the quantitative component of the study.

Quantitative component. Based on our literature review and interview results, we developed a survey, the Questionnaire on Disability Identity and Opportunity (QDIO). A copy of the questionnaire is included in the Appendix. The questionnaire was divided into two parts. The first part consisted of a thirty-item Likert scale with five response choices to measure the various dimensions of orientation to disability. Because the "direction" of the items was intentionally varied to avoid response patterning, in some cases a person with a particular attitude might agree with one item and disagree with another item measuring the same attitude. The second part consisted of fourteen questions that identified demographic and behavioral characteristics of the respondents. The instrument was designed to measure access and orientation. The dimensions of these concepts are:

• Access: to mainstream society and to the disability subculture.
• Orientation: identity (pride vs. stigma/shame), model (social vs. personal), and role (activism vs. passivity).

Although some individuals who have access to an activity may choose not to participate in it, for the purposes of our research, we operationalized *access* as participation. Clearly, a person can participate only in those activities to which he or she has access. Questions about participation were included in the second part of the QDIO, as well as in scale items. Examples of questions in this area include: "About how often do you engage in social activities outside of your home, like visiting friends or eating out in restaurants?" and "Please check the activities in which you participate at least once a month" (followed by a list of both mainstream activities and activities indicating participation in disability-related organizations).

Identity was operationalized through various scale items, including the following: "I don't think of myself as a person with a disability"; "My disability is an important part of who I am"; "I am proud of my disability"; "I try to hide my disability whenever I can." As these examples suggest, items reflected both disability pride and shame.

Model was operationalized through scale items such as the following: "All buildings should be accessible to people with disabilities"; "I feel sorry for people with disabilities"; "Doctors and other medical professionals know what is best for people with disabilities." As these examples suggest, some items suggested adherence to a social model, whereas others suggested adherence to a personal or medical model.

Finally, activism was operationalized primarily through the following question: "Have you ever participated in a demonstration, written a letter to your congressional representative, or engaged in another activity to try to increase the opportunities available to people with disabilities?" Passivity was suggested by lack of activism as well as by scale items such as, "The most important thing for people with disabilities is to learn to accept what they cannot change."

Among the orientations discussed in Chapter 6, typicality was expected to be reflected in agreement with items indicating access to mainstream society, rejection of disability pride and the social model, and a lack of activism. Agreement with items indicating access to the disability subculture and acceptance of disability pride (rejection of stigma), belief in the social model, and activism was expected to reflect the affirmative activism orientation. Personal activism was expected to be indicated by agreement with items indicating lack of access to mainstream society and acceptance of stigma, the personal model and activism. Finally, resignation was expected to be reflected in agreement with items indicating lack of access to both mainstream society and the disability subculture, acceptance of stigma and the personal model, and a rejection of activism. Isolated affirmative activism and apathy were not expected to be found in a sample drawn from the participants in disability-related organizations, and situational identification could not be measured by a survey conducted at a single point in time. However, these orientations should be considered in future research.

We distributed the QDIO anonymously with the assistance of four Centers for Independent Living, a social club and two assistance programs for people with disabilities, a rehabilitation facility, a posting on a disability website, and an Internet listserv for subscribers with disabilities. A total of 388 usable forms were returned from respondents in at least six states representing all regions of the United States. The data from these forms were analyzed using the techniques of factor and cluster analysis (using the Likert-scale items only), as well as cross-tabulations between the clusters that emerged and the demographic and behavioral items in the QDIO. The results of this analysis are reported in the next section.

Results

Qualitative component. Although our qualitative sample was small, we were able to identify disabled people who exhibited the orientations of typicality, affirmative activism, personal activism, and resignation. The following quotes are illustrative:

• Typicality: *Do you think of yourself as a person with a disability?* Not at all. *Why not?* I function real well. . . . I have a lot of family and my children, and there's nothing wrong with any of them. They don't consider me with a disability either.

• Affirmative activism: *What effect has your disability had on your life?* [If I didn't have a disability,] I think I would be a totally different person. . . . I am a better person. . . . I could never be that way if I were able-bodied.

• Resignation: *What effect has your disability had on your life?* Well, I just love to be out and among people, and it breaks my heart when I can't. I just. . . I know my limits but I wish I didn't have them, but, praise the Lord, he knows best.

• Personal activism: *Response to a follow-up question about the nature of an organization created by the respondent.* We're going to get all these doctors, hopefully, and we're going to give them an office booklet that explains the disease, . . . and, hopefully, it's going to make it a lot easier for people that have the disease, because the problem is the people who are supposed to know something about this stuff, they don't know anything about it. They don't know how to handle these people. . . . Five years, we're gonna have a treatment.

None of the qualitative responses suggested orientations that had not been considered previously. Because these orientations seemed to reflect those in the literature-based typology presented in Chapter 6, we ended this phase of the study after interviewing ten individuals and began the quantitative phase. In the section below, I describe the results of our analysis of the data from the QDIO.

Quantitative component. The 388 respondents in our sample ranged in age from young adults to those over 65, although younger adults predominated (median and modal ages were in the 18–35 age group). The sample included people from large urban areas, as well as from small towns and rural areas, but the majority came from small towns and small or medium-sized cities. A little more than half (54.3 percent) of the respondents were men. The most common type of impairment in the sample (46.3 percent) was mobility-related. Other impairments represented included vision (19.5 percent), hearing (16.5 percent), speech (16.2 percent), cognitive (25.7 percent), and cosmetic (4.9 percent) impairments. Obviously, some respondents had more than one. Like many samples of people with disabilities, these respondents generally had low incomes (68.6 percent had household incomes of under $25,000 a year) and were underemployed (only 20 percent worked full-time or were retired). Most people in the sample (83.6 percent) were European American, 8.3 percent identified themselves as African American, and the rest came from other racial backgrounds. A minority (17.5 percent) were college graduates, and the rest had less education. A large number (44.3 percent) had their disabilities since birth, an additional 24.3 percent had their disabilities for less than five years, and the remaining 31.4 percent fell somewhere in between.

Analysis of the data suggests that respondents had widely diverging orientations toward disability. The thirty-item scale was analyzed using exploratory factor analysis (EFA) to determine whether the items could be meaningfully grouped. The results of the factor analysis are reported in the next section. The data were then analyzed using k-means cluster analysis, based on the factors identified by the exploratory factor analysis, to determine whether respondents could be grouped in meaningful ways. In addition, clusters were cross-tabulated with responses to the behavioral and demographic items on the questionnaire to determine whether the types that emerged correlated with other characteristics in expected ways.

Exploratory factor analysis. Examination of the scree plot for the exploratory factor analysis of the thirty-item QDIO indicated that a four-factor solution was appropriate. Because we had reason to suspect that the four factors would be correlated, we ran the EFA using oblique rotation as well as varimax (orthogonal) rotation. Since the results were virtually identical with regard to which items loaded on the four factors, we present the results from the varimax rotation in Table 7.1. The four factors that emerged were disability pride; exclusion + dissatisfaction; social model; and personal/medical model. Based on item analysis, a few items were dropped for conceptual reasons or in the interests of parsimony (Preacher and MacCallum 2003). Reliability analyses revealed Cronbach's alpha levels (shown in Table 7.1) that were respectable for three of the subscales (disability pride = .78; exclusion/dissatisfaction = .73; social model = .72), and marginally acceptable for the personal/medical model subscale (alpha = .63) (DeVellis 1991). Although the alpha coefficients are not as high as desirable, we judged them to be acceptable given the relatively small number of items in the subscales and the fact that we used self-report administration of the survey, which may have presented challenges for some of the participants. Although the survey was designed for self-report, we suspect, based on anecdotal evidence, that a small number of participants from the rehabilitation facility that contributed to the sample may have had low levels of literacy, which may have resulted in some misunderstanding of survey items.

Cluster analysis. Unlike factor analysis, which groups scale *items* based on similar response patterns among participants, cluster analysis groups *participants* based on common responses to scale items. The cluster analysis was based on the four factors derived from the factor analysis, sorting the sample according to common factor affinities. A six-cluster solution was determined to be the most interpretable. These clusters largely reflected four of the types in the theoretical typology described in the last chapter: typicality (30 percent of the sample, divided into two clusters as explained below), personal activism (21 percent of the sample), affirmative activism (11 percent of the sample), and resignation (16 percent of the sample), although not in all proposed dimensions. The remaining cluster (22 percent of the sample) tended to be neutral with regard to all four factors. Table 7.2 shows the cluster centers for each factor.

The original typology included ideal types, which, like all ideal

Table 7.1 Summary of Exploratory Factor Analysis Results for the QDIO Using Varimax Rotation (N = 388)

	Factor 1	Factor 2	Factor 3	Factor 4
Disability pride; alpha = .78				
I am a better person because of my disability.	**.531**	.160	−.129	.016
My disability is an important part of who I am.	**.613**	.131	−.091	−.072
I am proud of my disability.	**.635**	.033	−.194	−.103
My disability enriches my life.	**.706**	.059	−.209	−.069
Exclusion/dissatisfaction; alpha = .73				
My disability limits my social life.	−.014	.194	**.677**	.010
My disability keeps me from working.	−.043	.170	**.594**	.133
In general, I am satisfied with the quality of my life (reversed).	−.486	.064	**.496**	−.178
I often am excluded from activities because of my disability.	−.073	.408	**.556**	−.066
Social model; alpha = .72				
Lack of accessibility and discrimination by employers are the main reasons why disabled people are unemployed.	.069	**.590**	−.017	.019
It isn't easy for people with disabilities to be treated as "normal."	−.031	**.430**	.163	.118
People with disabilities need to fight for their rights more than nondisabled people do.	.038	**.555**	.097	.092
The biggest problem faced by people with disabilities is the attitudes of other people.	.082	**.596**	.127	.036
All buildings should be accessible to people with disabilities.	.095	**.537**	−.064	.093
I am familiar with the Americans with Disabilities Act (ADA) and think it is a good law.	.198	**.398**	−.043	−.039
I am familiar with the Disability Rights Movement and support its goals.	.228	**.427**	−.025	−.021
Personal/medical model; alpha = .63				
If I had a choice, I would prefer not to have a disability.	−.269	.213	.120	**.346**
I feel sorry for people with disabilities.	−.093	−.060	.179	**.421**
I wish that someone would find a cure for my disability.	−.219	.311	.319	**.416**
Doctors and other medical professionals know what is best for people with disabilities.	.175	.002	.058	**.474**
People with disabilities need to learn to adjust to living in a world in which most people are not disabled.	.024	.124	.067	**.353**
I try to hide my disability whenever I can.	−.042	−.072	.351	**.406**
People should try to overcome their disabilities.	−.100	.067	−.109	**.398**
The most important thing for people with disabilities is to learn to accept what they cannot change.	.135	.044	−.120	**.410**
Eigenvalues	4.11	3.91	2.12	1.74
% of variance	13.7	13.0	7.07	5.78

Note: Items that loaded with each of the four factors are indicated in **bold**.

Table 7.2 Cluster Centers and Their Meaning for Each Factor

Factor	Cluster					
	1 Resignation	2 Normative Typicality	3 Personal Activism	4	5 Affirmative Activism	6 Affirmative Typicality
Disability pride	Disagree/ strongly disagree (4.17)	Disagree/ strongly disagree (4.13)	Agree/ not sure (2.26)	Disagree/ not sure (3.62)	Agree/ strongly agree (1.61)	Not sure/ agree (2.67)
Exclusion	Agree/ strongly agree (1.81)	Disagree/ strongly disagree (4.24)	Not sure/ agree (2.61)	Not sure (3.05)	Disagree/ strongly disagree (4.18)	Disagree/ strongly disagree (4.24)
Social model	Agree (2.02)	Not sure/ agree (2.83)	Agree/ strongly agree (1.77)	Agree/ not sure (2.22)	Agree/ strongly agree (1.84)	Agree/ not sure (2.42)
Personal model	Agree/ not sure (2.31)	Not sure (3.06)	Agree/ not sure (2.41)	Agree/ not sure (2.46)	Disagree/ not sure (3.35)	Agree/ not sure (2.44)

types in sociology, only approximate actual orientations. Consequently, we were unsurprised to find that our respondents showed some response variability and were not "perfect" examples of the types they closely approximated.

Cross-tabulations. Most of the demographic and behavioral items included in the questionnaire were significantly associated with cluster. The only items with no association were gender, race, attendance at religious services, telephone conversations with friends and family, and the nature of the place where they lived (rural versus urban). This finding is not surprising, given the general lack of theoretical connection between any of these items and the variables being measured in this study. (As I noted in Chapter 4, race may be associated to some extent with disability identity, but this association was not supported in this study, perhaps because the number of African American respondents was small and unrepresentative.)

The other items were all significantly associated with cluster (chi squares with p < .000 except for income, for which p < .03). Table 7.3 shows the dominant characteristics of each cluster based on the cross-tabulations.

As Table 7.3 suggests, cluster 4 showed no tendencies in the cross-tabulations that were remarkable; rather, these respondents tended to fall somewhere in the middle on all items, just as they had on the scale items that determined the clusters. We suspect that this group either had difficulty in understanding the questionnaire or chose to respond in random ways. The inclusion in the sample of people with cognitive disabilities may account for this finding to some extent. However, because of the anonymity of respondents, we are unable to confirm or deny this possibility. Because this cluster was completely unremarkable, the following analysis will focus on clusters 1, 2, 3, 5, and 6 only.

Discussion

The factor and cluster analyses and cross-tabulations support the literature-based typology of disability orientations to a large extent. Below, I describe each of the ideal types that emerged from our analyses and then compare them with respect to the components of disability orientation (identity, role, and model) presented in Chapter 6. These descriptions reflect statistical tendencies and are not intended to describe actual respondents.

Affirmative typicality (cluster 6). This group is marked by a high level of inclusion in mainstream society. They are socially active and have the highest income of any of the clusters. They tend to be younger, and many are students. Although they have had their disabilities since birth, they are not very disabled, as indicated by their low level of need for assistance with daily activities. Although they use the Internet, they do not visit disability-related websites or participate in disability-related activism. However, they do not reject or deny their identity as individuals with disabilities. They do not strongly identify with either the social or the personal model.

Normative typicality (cluster 2). This group is similar to the affirmative typicality group in that they are younger, they are included in mainstream society, and they are not very disabled. Similarly, they do not strongly support either the social or the personal model of disability and do not engage in disability-related activism. However, unlike the first typicality cluster, they are likely to have acquired their disability after birth and to reject an identity of disability pride.

Affirmative activism (cluster 5). Like the typicality clusters, this cluster shows a high level of inclusion in mainstream society and is the most likely to be employed. These respondents tend to be younger,

Table 7.3 Dominant Demographic and Behavioral Characteristics of Each Cluster

		Cluster			
1 Resignation	2 Normative Typicality	3 Personal Activism	4	5 Affirmative Activism	6 Affirmative Typicality
Older	Younger			Younger	Younger
Mostly retired or unemployed	Mostly students	Mostly unemployed or students		Most likely to be employed full- or part-time (34.9%)	Mostly students
Least educated				Most highly educated (40.9% college graduates)	
Mostly mobility-impaired	Most not mobility-impaired				Most not mobility-impaired
Most have acquired disability	Somewhat likely to have aquired disability	Most have disability since birth		Most have disability since birth	Most have disability since birth
Most need for assistance with ADLs	Least need for assistance with ADLs				Least need for assistance with ADLs
Least socially active	Somewhat socially active	Less socially active		Most socially active	Most socially active
Least likely to engage in disability activism	Least likely to engage in disability activism	Most likely to engage in disability activism		Most likely to engage in disability activism	Least likely to engage in disability activism
Most do not use e-mail	Somewhat likely to use e-mail	Somewhat likely to use e-mail		Most likely to use e-mail	
Unlikely to visit disability websites	Unlikely to visit disability websites	Somewhat unlikely to visit disability websites		Most likely to visit disability websites	Unlikely to visit disability websites
Unlikely to visit other websites	Likely to visit other websites	Somewhat unlikely to visit other websites		Likely to visit other websites	Likely to visit other websites
Unlikely to attend disability-related meetings	Unlikely to attend disability-related meetings			Most likely to attend disability-related meetings	Unlikely to attend disability-related meetings
	Unlikely to read disability-related magazines				Unlikely to read disability-related magazines
Lowest income ($p < .029$)					Highest income ($p < .029$)

Notes: ADLs are activities of daily living. P-values for X^2 values for all variables are $< .000$, except for income ($p < .029$). Full cross-tabulation results are available upon request.

and many have graduated from college. They are socially active and use both e-mail and the Internet, as well as attending meetings of disability-related organizations. They are the most likely of any of the clusters to engage in disability activism. They favor the social model over the personal model and are the most likely of any cluster to have an identity of disability pride. Most have had their disabilities since birth.

Personal activism (cluster 3). Although not as activist as the affirmative activism cluster, these respondents also prefer the social model and do engage in a considerable amount of disability activism. However, unlike the affirmative activism cluster, they are somewhat likely to be excluded from mainstream society and are mostly unemployed and less socially active. Most have had their disabilities since birth and have some disability pride.

Resignation (cluster 1). These respondents are the oldest of any of the clusters. They also are the least educated and have the lowest incomes. They are the most likely to be excluded from mainstream society and are the least socially active. They are the most disabled of any of the clusters and are likely to have acquired their disabilities later in life. They do not use the Internet and do not engage in disability activism. They were the most likely to agree with the personal/medical model of disability and to reject disability pride.

The emergence of two typicality clusters is not surprising. As N. Watson (2002), Gilson and Depoy (2004) and others have suggested, some individuals who achieve typicality do not deny their identities as people with disabilities, an orientation that describes our first typicality cluster (affirmative typicality). Others who achieve typicality (normative typicality), however, do appear to accept the societal norm of stigma and to reject the notion of disability pride. Interestingly, all the clusters that had their disabilities since birth seemed comfortable enough with their identities to agree with items suggesting disability pride. Both clusters that had acquired their disabilities later in life, however, accepted the societal norm of stigma, as indicated by their rejection of disability pride.

To summarize our findings relating to the major variables of the study, we developed a table characterizing each cluster accordingly. Table 7.4 compares the five orientations above in terms of four major variables: identity (pride versus stigma); access (inclusion versus exclusion from mainstream society); model (personal versus social), and role (activism versus passivity).

Table 7.4 suggests that lack of access to opportunities for social participation may be a determinant of activism for those with a personal activism orientation. For the individuals in the personal activism category, activism may be a way of attempting to acquire opportunities for inclusion in mainstream society that are already available to those in the affirmative activism category. The latter group, however, appear to be activists for more altruistic reasons, as they already have achieved inclusion for themselves. They may become involved and remain active in the disability rights movement or disability-related organizations as a way of showcasing their pride and/or creating social change for other people with disabilities. Moreover, the relationships that develop within movements and organizations may serve to sustain their membership and associated activism. A. Asch (2004) has asserted that her continued involvement in disability rights activism grows out of her sense of injustice and her friendships within the movement. Although she does not view her disability negatively, she rejects the notion of disability pride. Clearly, pride exists on a continuum among affirmers, yet all seem to reject stigma or shame.

Lack of opportunities for social participation does not appear to be an impetus to activism for those in the resignation category. These individuals had the most significant disabilities of any of the clusters, and most had acquired their disabilities later in life. Perhaps they were too involved in issues of rehabilitation or coping to engage in activism. Activism, after all, is time-consuming and requires at least a minimal level of energy. Those who are older and who have less education also are less likely to use the Internet or to have access to the disability subculture described in Chapter 6.

Degree of disability also seems to have some bearing on activism. Interestingly, the most (resignation) and the least (typicality)

Table 7.4 Characteristics of Each Orientation for Four Variables

Orientation	Identity	Access	Model	Role
Normative typicality	Stigma	Inclusion	No preference	Passive
Affirmative typicality	Some pride	Inclusion	No preference	Passive
Affirmative activism	Pride	Inclusion	Social	Activist
Personal activism	Some pride	Exclusion	Social	Activist
Resignation	Stigma	Exclusion	No preference	Passive

disabled clusters had the lowest levels of activism. As opportunity structure theory would suggest, those with less significant disabilities may be better able to fit into mainstream society and thus to identify with mainstream norms rather than those of the disability subculture, whereas those with the most significant disabilities may not have access to *either* mainstream society *or* the disability subculture.

Although the affirmative activism cluster had the highest level of disability pride, disability identity appears to be unrelated to activism in general. Rather, the primary determinant of identity seems to be whether or not one is born with a disability. People with lifelong disabilities learn from an early age to feel comfortable with their identity, whereas those who acquire disabilities later in life have already been socialized into the societal norm of stigma. This finding contradicts the expectation, based on the literature review and the qualitative component of the study, that all but those in the affirmative activism cluster would reject disability pride, but supports the association reported by H. D. Hahn and T. L. Belt (2004) between positive disability identity and early age of disability onset. Thus, the presence of disability pride cannot be explained by adherence to the social model alone.

One additional finding in this study did not strongly support our expectations. *All* the clusters agreed to some extent with the social model (factor 3), although some (affirmative activists and personal activists) agreed more strongly than others. Perhaps most people with disabilities today have been exposed to the message of the disability rights movement, or perhaps our measure needs to be refined to discriminate better among clusters. The personal/medical model factor, which had the lowest alpha, may also need more refinement, although the clusters tended to be associated with it in predictable ways, with the affirmative activists disagreeing with it the most and the resigned agreeing with it the most.

Thus, an understanding of disability orientation seems to involve all the postulated elements: identity, access, model, and role. Model and role seem to be associated in predicted ways, whereas identity seems to depend more on whether one's disability is acquired after birth than on model. Access appears to be associated with the presence or absence of activism in more complex ways. Those in the resignation cluster do not engage in activism, even though they lack access to opportunities for inclusion in mainstream society, yet they also appear to lack access to opportunities for learning about activism.

Clearly, further research, especially of a qualitative nature, is needed to establish the accuracy of the explanations offered here. In particular, future research needs to explore the processes through which people come to adopt various orientations toward disability. However, the findings of this study suggest that the process of becoming an activist depends to some extent on both personal (nature of the disability) and social (access to opportunities) factors.

Implications of the Study

The study's findings provide a limited test of the existence of the social model of disability and suggest that both the personal and the social models are present to varying degrees in various segments of the population of people with disabilities in the United States today. The study also raises some interesting questions about the interaction between opportunities and orientations.

Opportunity structure theory appears to be supported in part by the research. The typicality clusters, which have access to mainstream society, seem to reject disability activism. The personal activism cluster's activism and fairly strong identification with the social model may be motivated by a lack of opportunities for inclusion. The affirmative activism cluster appears to reject mainstream views of disability, regardless of opportunities for inclusion, because they identify strongly with the social model of the disability subculture. Finally, the resignation cluster, like R. K. Merton's (1949) "retreatism" category, seems to consist of people who lack access to both mainstream society and to the disability subculture.

Although the results of the study are promising, further research is needed to test our instrument and our findings with a randomly selected, representative sample. The convenience sample used here included an overrepresentation of young adults and of students, mostly from a large rehabilitation center. In addition, the sample included an overrepresentation of nonurban and low-income respondents. Nevertheless, the fact that the clusters were associated with most of the variables predicted by theory provides evidence of the convergent validity of the clusters. In addition, the fact that interpretable clusters were derived from the four factors generated from the factor analysis provides evidence that the four QDIO subscales are valid as well. In other analyses, we found further evidence of convergent validity, as age was negatively associated with disability pride and positively associated with exclusion, as predicted by theory. I further explore the findings related to age in the next chapter. A next step for future research would be to validate the QDIO with a larger and more representative sample of people with disabilities. The validated instrument would then serve as the basis for a large-scale study using a national or international sample to determine the proportion of people in the population who adhere to each of the orientations identified. The association of orientation with quality of life is also an important area for future research.

In addition to further quantitative research, qualitative studies are needed to explain how individuals come to adopt various orientations and how these orientations may change over time in relation to the presence or absence of various interactional opportunities. Increased knowledge about the career paths of individuals with disabilities would be valuable for practitioners and policy makers in their work to increase opportunities for this population.

Future research in this area would have important practical applications. In addition to increasing scholarly knowledge about the population of people with disabilities, the QDIO could be used by practitioners to learn more about the disability orientations of particular individuals. Although further research will help us more fully understand the relationship between disability orientation and quality of life, the research reported here suggests that some orientations (typicality and affirmative activism) produce greater life satisfaction than others, perhaps because of more opportunities for inclusion in mainstream society. A better understanding of disability orientation might result in interventions to promote those orientations that are associated with a better quality of life. In addition, policymakers need to be aware of the diversity of orientations toward disability when developing legislation or programs. Social policy can increase or decrease opportunities for social inclusion. The research reported here represents a first step in broadening knowledge in an important yet understudied area.

Conclusion

In this chapter I presented the results of an empirical study that attempted to test the typology presented in Chapter 6. The study suggested that at least five ideal-typical orientations toward disability appear to be present: affirmative typicality (typicality with positive disability identity), normative typicality (typicality without pride), personal activism; affirmative activism, and resignation. Although these are ideal types that are only approximated by actual individuals, they clearly support the argument that disability identity and orientation are diverse in US society today.

Note

This chapter is a revised version of Rosalyn Benjamin Darling and D. Alex Heckert, "Activism, Models, Identities, and Opportunities: A Preliminary Test of a Typology of Disability Orientations," *Research in Social Science and Disability* 5 (2010): 203–229.

8

Identity over the Life Course

As I showed in Chapter 7, identities and orientations toward disability are diverse. Moreover, an individual may have a different identity or orientation at different points in time as a result of interactions with new individuals or groups. For example, a person with a resignation orientation might adopt the orientation of affirmative activism after an encounter with a disability rights' activist. Whether disability orientation careers are patterned is an interesting question that needs to be addressed by a longitudinal study. However, one of the significant findings of the study described in Chapter 7 was the association between age and disability orientation. Both chronological age and age at disability onset appear to be important in shaping one's orientation toward disability. I explore these associations further in this chapter, focusing on the identities of children and adults with early onset disabilities and on disability identity in old age.

Identity Negotiation Among Children and Young Adults with Disabilities

The literature review in Chapter 3 showed that children with disabilities tend to have positive self-concepts, with levels of self-esteem that do not differ significantly from those of their nondisabled peers. Symbolic interaction theory suggests that they learn these self-views in reference groups that filter or protect them from the stigma present in the larger society. In addition, a number of studies have shown that children are not merely the passive recipients of definitions from others; they negotiate their environments to maintain their self-esteem. In symbolic interaction terms, they *role-play* and engage in *self-presentation* in their interactions with other people.

Most children with disabilities have not been exposed to the social model of disability. Because of their parents' focus on maximizing their abilities through medical or therapeutic intervention, many have become well acquainted with medical settings and the models on which they are based (Connors and Stalker 2007). They have learned from an early age that their bodies need "repair." Not surprisingly then, in interviews with university students, L. Middleton (1999, 9) found that most of them attributed the negative experiences in their lives to their impairments, and many did not have a positive disability identity. She found further that many reported that others had low expectations of them during childhood, and many had been "belittled, bullied, and abused," resulting in ongoing threats to their self-esteem. Yet they apparently managed to be successful enough to enter a university, suggesting some ability to overcome their early devaluation.

Although the young people in many studies view their impairments through the lens of the medical model, they do not typically see them as "tragedies." When C. Connors and K. Stalker (2007) asked their respondents whether they would change anything about themselves if they could, only a few mentioned their impairments. Most seemed to view their impairments as natural parts of their identities.

In in-depth interviews with a small sample of deaf children, M. Sheridan (2001, 219) found that most of the children had strong, positive self-views, regardless of the definitions they had received from some others. The children seemed to be able to compartmentalize definitions received from "domesticated others" (those perceived as accepting) and "disparate others," with whom the children were less comfortable. Sheridan reports that the children developed "positive *pathways* for negotiating their relationships with disparate others," including isolating themselves from situations in which barriers existed and taking the initiative to structure situations in ways that enabled them to participate. In general, the children saw their deafness as "no big deal."

Similarly, M. Priestley (1999, 98) found that the disabled British high school students he interviewed did not passively accept negative definitions they received from others and "were by no means passive in the construction of their identities within the school context." Although the children rejected negative disability labels placed upon them by other students, they sometimes chose to emphasize a disabled identity in interactions with school authorities to avoid homework assignments, for example. Priestley explains, "[The students were] happy to play out the 'disabled' role when they thought it would be a successful negotiating tactic. . . . However, . . . this was invariably done with a high degree of irony and self-awareness" (101). He argues that, as social actors, these students negotiate their identities in ways they perceive as advantageous.

A review of several studies of school-aged children and young adults with disabilities reveals a prominent theme of typicality. Connors and Stalker (2007) and others have noted that the children they interviewed saw themselves as not very different from their nondisabled peers. Similarly, J. Low (1996, 240) noted in a study of college students with disabilities that "uppermost in their minds is negotiating a non-disabled identity." In a study of children dependent on medical technology, S. Kirk (2010, 1798) found that "Young people developed strategies to manage their condition, the technology and their identities in order to incorporate the technology into their lives and bodies and 'live an ordinary life'. This required continual work in response to changing social contexts and relationships." In their descriptions of themselves, these children emphasized their participation in "normal" activities such as sports and outings to clubs.

In order to present a normalized self to others, Kirk's respondents developed a variety of strategies, such as timing medical procedures so that they would not interfere with other activities. Some engaged in covering or passing, and many selectively revealed their conditions to only a few trusted friends. The students Low studied employed techniques such as using humor, avoiding confrontations, reasoning, and trying to be inconspicuous. Many of Low's respondents also distanced themselves from other students with disabilities.

In a Swedish study of young adults with intellectual disabilities, E. Olin and B. R. Jansson (2009) found a number of orientations. The "pragmatic navigators" had a typicality orientation to a large extent. They described themselves in positive terms and enjoyed life. Most avoided telling other people about their disabilities because they believed that others would underestimate their competence and abilities. Like the respondents in the other studies described in this section, they negotiated their environments to avoid situations they did not believe they could manage. They did not deny their disabilities or their limitations but presented themselves in a way that would maximize their opportunities for a "normal" life. They "provided an image of themselves as 'different but normal'" (263).

Thus, most of the literature on young people with disabilities suggests that the affirmative typicality orientation described in Chapter 7 is most common. These individuals do not reject a disability identity, but they work hard to fit in with "normal" society and tend to minimize the role played by their disabilities in everyday life. Other young people described in these studies seem to fit more closely with the normative typicality orientation; they choose not to think of themselves as disabled and avoid associating with other disabled individuals.

The literature also includes some evidence of other orientations in this population. Olin and Jansson (2009) describe some of their respondents as "critical challengers." Young people in this group are dissatisfied with their lives and tend to blame society for their difficulties. They fight continuously for recognition of their rights. This group seems to exemplify the personal activism orientation described in Chapter 7.

Finally, Olin and Jansson (2009) describe some of their respondents as "misunderstood rebels." Like some with a typicality orientation, these individuals deny their disabilities, yet they are unable to fit into "normal" society. Their exclusion resembles the situation of those with a resignation orientation described in Chapter 7.

The one orientation conspicuously absent among the young people in all these studies is affirmative activism. L. Middleton (1999, 27) notes with respect to the university students in her study: "Only one of the respondents was conscious of being exposed to disability rights literature or activism. They did not use words like 'rights', 'control', 'choice' or 'respect'. Their ambitions took the form of wishing to belong, to be valued, to mix with able-bodied people as well as in a disabled world, and to be understood." Connors and Stalker (2007, 30) argue that the children they studied "did not have a language with which to discuss difference." As a result, they could not apply a social model framework to their experiences of exclusion. As noted earlier in this book, children with disabilities tend not to have disabled adults as role models and, consequently, do not encounter ideas about affirmation and the social model until later in life, if at all.

Although most of these children and young adults have had their disabilities from an early age, a few do acquire disabilities as a result of injury or illness later in childhood or adolescence. L. Jemta and colleagues (2009) found a lower level of psychological well-being in the children and adolescents in their study who had acquired their disabilities later in their lives. In this respect, they resemble some of the adults with later onset disability, who will be discussed later in this chapter.

Aging with a Preexisting Disability

Because most children with disabilities appear to adopt a typicality orientation, they are likely to maintain that orientation in adulthood as long as they continue to have opportunities for inclusion in "normal" activities, such as employment and social relationships. Those who experience discrimination or stigma, however, may become politicized after an encounter with a disability rights activist. The processes through which politicization occurs were described in earlier chapters.

L. M. Verbrugge and L.-S. Yang (2002) distinguish between "aging with disability" and "disability with aging." Disability increases with age. Although most older adults with disabilities have acquired their disabilities later in life, an increasing proportion of the aging population includes individuals with early onset disabilities, who have aged with disability (Verbrugge and Yang 2002). M. Minkler and P. Fadem (2002) argue that paradigms of "successful aging" in gerontology tend to view disability negatively and need to be broadened to include those with pre-existing disabilities who are "aging well." However, little research has focused on the correlates of "successful aging" among people with disabilities over the life course. Moreover, as M. Putnam (2002) suggests, newer social models of disability need to be integrated into theories of aging.

One group that has received some research attention as its members have aged is the deaf community. In the past, especially, many members of this community attended special schools where they developed friendship networks with others like themselves. Y. Bat-Chava (1994) found that those who grew up in environments that included other deaf people and sign language were more likely to identify with the deaf community in adulthood. This identification was associated with positive self-esteem, whereas those who did not identify with the deaf community had low self-esteem. Because this community is linguistically and culturally distinct, its members learn alternative views of themselves and their deafness that insulate them to some extent from the stigma of the larger society.

In a classic study of deaf people in old age, G. Becker (1980, 40) found that her respondents "defined themselves primarily in terms of deafness." She writes, "Deafness plays such a pivotal role in the self-concept of deaf people that at times it completely obscures the fact that the person has other attributes." The centrality of their deafness results from continual reminders from the larger society that they are outsiders.

> By old age individual identity processes have undergone significant changes. Nevertheless, the day-to-day realities of being deaf continue to affect one's identity. Throughout life the deaf person is in a continual identity conflict, made explicit in interactions with hearing people because these interactions call attention to the deaf person's inadequacies. . . .
>
> Interaction with other deaf people, on the other hand, tends to reinforce positive feelings about one's abilities and validates one's worth as an individual. . . . In old age the individual's identity as a deaf person . . . provides a sense of connectedness and fends off feelings of worthlessness, alienation, and isolation. (40–41, 100–101)

One of the ways the deaf community validates its members' self-esteem is by emphasizing sociability over achievement. A close-knit peer group provides friendship, mutual aid, and, importantly, an alternative worldview, in which deafness is not a negative attribute. Becker concludes that the "aged deaf share a collective identity with all other deaf people. Their collective identity is based on a status devalued by disability. They have legitimized their status in their own eyes through the normalization process" (107).

Some individuals with disabilities other than deafness also maintain their self-esteem over the life course through immersion in a community of peers. As I explained in earlier chapters, these individuals tend to adopt a personal activism or a typicality orientation. Studies suggest, however, that typicality continues to be the most common orientation of individuals with early onset disabilities, regardless of age.

In some cases, a preexisting disability may become more pronounced with age. For example, some polio survivors experience postpolio syndrome in their later years. D. J. Wilson (2004, 131–132) offers the example of someone who "discovers that as post-polio imposes new limits on his body, he can face the decline with the greater 'equanimity' gained from the experience of a lifetime." Like the aging deaf people described above, and unlike people who acquire new disabilities later in life, this individual and others like him may be able to adapt with little difficulty to changes associated with aging.

A small British study of deinstitutionalized, older (over age 50) adults with Down syndrome (Brown et al. 2009) found that neither Down syndrome nor disability was part of their respondents' identities. Instead, these individuals focused on their gender, social roles, and physical characteristics. One described himself as "a normal man" (221). These identities suggest typicality without disability pride (normative typicality). However, as S. Beart and colleagues (2005) noted in a literature review of studies of identity among people with intellectual disabilities, some members of this population may not have the cognitive ability to understand their label, and others' lived experiences may have shielded them from the label and its stigma.

Later Onset Disability

Those who acquire their disabilities later in life seem to prefer typicality as well, but this orientation may be elusive for them. Most have a strong identity as a nondisabled person when they acquire a disability. Generally, they have interacted in groups of other nondisabled people and have been exposed to societal stigma and stereotypes regarding people with disabilities, along with the prevailing medical model. As a result, the acquisition of a disability during adulthood is commonly viewed negatively. Not surprisingly, as most disabilities are acquired and not inborn, studies of older adults (see, e.g., V. A. Freedman 2012) have found that having a disability is associated with a lower sense of well-being.

Robert Murphy (Murphy 1990, 85), who acquired quadriplegia in middle age, writes, "I had lost much more than the full use of my legs. I had also lost a part of my self." He explains that the effects on his self-esteem of his bodily changes were magnified by the negative reactions of others and argues that disability is a master status that overshadows other aspects of the self: "A serious disability inundates all other claims to social standing, relegating to secondary status all the attainments of life. . . . It is an identity . . . to which all social roles must be adjusted" (101). He expresses considerable anger about his loss of self-esteem and his new "undesirable" identity. Similarly, in a posting on a disability studies listserv (SDS 2007), someone wrote,

> I've encountered a schism regarding the term disability pride which seems to at least in part lie between those with disabilities acquired later in life and those who were born with them. . . . The idea of pride in disability seems to be most foreign among those people I know who have spinal cord injuries. . . . I hear things like what do I have to be proud of? I didn't ask for this and don't want it, I hate being SCI [*sic*] why would I want to celebrate it?

K. Lindgren (2004, 155) suggests that biomedical and popular images view illness or disability as alien to the body, making it likely that "we will imagine [it] as an other within the self." As a result, she argues, a disability acquired in adulthood can threaten "an established sense of self." She uses autobiographical accounts to show how a newly acquired disability "estranges the person with disabilities from his social world," a reaction that also characterized some of the accounts presented in earlier chapters of this book.

K. Charmaz (1999) points out that the self often changes as a result of turning points, at which new information is acquired. For example, experiencing stigma for the first time after acquiring a disability may have an impact on a person's self-concept. She notes, however, that the sense of loss that follows such a turning point is not always permanent. Many are able to reevaluate their loss and redefine it in positive terms. Charmaz cites cases of people who came to see their new selves as stronger and more resilient than their old ones. I found similar processes among the parents of children with disabilities I interviewed. Most were initially overcome with grief but later came to believe that they were "better people" as a result of having to adapt to a difficult situation.

Using the concept of "identity goals" to describe changes in self-concept following the acquisition of a chronic illness or disability, Charmaz (1995) argues that, alongside their present identities, people envision themselves in the future and act to realize their goals. Such self-planning may be drastically altered by the experience of disability. For example, a man who anticipated being his family's breadwinner through construction work might have to reassess his ability to perform that role after acquiring a significant physical disability. Charmaz points out that conflicts with partners may occur during the reassessment process and the resulting interactions may affect one's self and identity goals. As a result, "identity trade-offs" occur, and the disabled person may choose to emphasize some identity goals over others.

Thus, "time with disability" appears to be an important variable. Some individuals with acquired disabilities may eventually have typicality or affirmative activism orientations after coming to terms with their losses. L. A. Schur (1998) found that the highly politically active respondents with spinal cord injuries that she studied tended to be older and to have lived with their injuries for a longer period of time. She argues that those who have lived with their injuries longer have had more opportunity to experience stigma, resulting in politicization. Of course, they also have had more time to encounter a disability rights' activist and to revise their identity goals.

A few studies have looked specifically at self-identification as disabled. L. I. Iezzoni and colleagues (2000) found that although most people with major mobility difficulties perceived themselves as disabled, almost 30 percent did not. J. A. Kelley-Moore and colleagues (2006) found that among older people, self-identification as disabled was associated with changes in social networks and other variables such as cessation of driving and receipt of home health care, and not simply with the acquisition of functional limitations. Similarly, J. A. Langlois and colleagues (1996) have reported that 61 percent of older adults who had difficulty with or could not perform at least one activity of daily living did not consider themselves to be disabled, suggesting a normative typicality orientation.

The relationship between disability orientation and age has hardly been explored in the empirical literature. One study (Hahn and Belt 2004) looked at disability identity in relation to age of disability onset in a sample of disability activists. The authors found that personal affirmation of disability was stronger among those with early onset disability than among those with adult onset. However, they do not report any findings relating these variables to the age of their respondents. In order to further explore the relationship between age and disability orientation, D. A. Heckert and I (Darling and Heckert 2010b) reanalyzed the data from the study reported in Chapter 7. Our findings are described in the next section.

An Empirical Study of Age and Disability Orientation

Data Analysis and Findings

In addition to the factor analysis reported in Chapter 7, we cross-tabulated each of the items on the QDIO with age. Table 8.1 presents the measures of statistical association between all thirty Likert items and age using Somer's D with age (since the items and age are measured at the ordinal level), along with other items on the QDIO that were associated with age (based on a statistically significant Somer's D value). Although most of the bivariate associations with age were weak to moderate, some interesting patterns became evident. Specifically, the results suggest that older people are more likely to espouse a medical model (e.g., desiring a cure, believing that "doctors know best"), to feel excluded from social participation (e.g., disability keeps them from working and limits their social life), and to reject an identity of disability pride (although they are more likely to think of themselves as disabled, they do not view this identity in positive terms). In addition, life satisfaction decreases with age. Disability rights activism shows a curvilinear relationship with age: Adults aged 36–64 are the most activist, with more than half having engaged in some form of disability rights activism, whereas younger adults and those over 65 are less activist. Interestingly, age was negatively associated with length of time with a disability: young adults in our sample were more likely to be disabled from birth and to have their disability for a longer period of time.

We computed mean subscale scores for the four factors—disability pride (4 items), exclusion/dissatisfaction (4 items), the social model (7 items), and the personal/medical model (8 items)—with high scores reflecting agreement with each of these factors (see Table 7.1 for the specific items used in each subscale). As shown in Table 8.2, we then performed a multiple analysis of variance (MANOVA) on the four factors with age as the independent variable. The results revealed a significant relationship ($p < .000$) between age and Factor 1 (disability pride) and between age and Factor 2 (exclusion). Younger respondents were more likely to agree with the items associated with disability pride and to have higher average scores on disability pride. Older respondents were more likely to agree with the items associated with exclusion, and to report perceiving higher average levels of exclusion/dissatisfaction.

Table 8.1 Bivariate Relationships Between Age and QDIO Items and Nonscale Items (*N* = 388)

	Somer's D
Disability pride	
I am a better person because of my disability.	–.16[b]
My disability is an important part of who I am.	–.20[c]
I am proud of my disability.	–.29[c]
My disability enriches my life.	–.16[b]
Exclusion/dissatisfaction	
My disability limits my social life.	.44[c]
My disability keeps me from working.	.37[c]
In general, I am satisfied with the quality of my life. (reversed)	–.34[c]
I often am excluded from activities because of my disability.	.33[c]
Social model	
Lack of accessibility and discrimination by employers are the main reasons why disabled people are unemployed.	.06
It isn't easy for people with disabilities to be treated as "normal."	–.03
People with disabilities need to fight for their rights more than nondisabled people do.	.09
The biggest problem faced by people with disabilities is the attitudes of other people.	.04
All buildings should be accessible to people with disabilities.	.04
I am familiar with the Americans with Disabilities Act (ADA) and think it is a good law.	.14[b]
I am familiar with the Disability Rights Movement and support its goals.	.07
Personal/medical model	
If I had a choice, I would prefer not to have a disability.	.23[c]
I feel sorry for people with disabilities.	–.09
I wish that someone would find a cure for my disability.	.23[c]
Doctors and other medical professionals know what is best for people with disabilities.	.13[a]
People with disabilities need to learn to adjust to living in a world…	.11[a]
I try to hide my disability whenever I can.	.10
People should try to overcome their disabilities.	.06
The most important thing for people with disabilities is to learn to accept what they cannot change.	.08
Other QDIO items and significant nonscale items	
I don't think of myself as a disabled person.	–.22[c]
I would rather associate with disabled people than people without disabilities.	.07
Most of my friends have disabilities.	–.31[c]
The reason most people with disabilities are unemployed is that they are not able to do the jobs that are available.	.05
I have a lot in common with other people with disabilities.	.06
People with disabilities can never fit into "normal" society.	–.004
The people I care about always include me in activities I am able to enjoy.	.14[b]
Mobility impairments	.44[c]
Time with disability	–.35[c]
Need for assistance with ADLs	.38[c]
Social participation	–.31[c]
Disability rights activism (not linear)	–.13[b]
Use of e-mail/internet	–.18[c]
Read disability magazines (not linear)	–.18[c]

Notes: a. *p* < .05
b. *p* < .01
c. *p* < .001

Table 8.2 Means of Disability Factors by Age Categories

	18–35 years $N = 217$	36–64 years $N = 136$	65+ years $N = 35$	Type III SS	F-Value	Significance
Pride	3.14$_a$	2.73$_b$	2.32$_c$	25.54	13.06	.000
Exclusion	2.30$_a$	3.28$_b$	3.45$_b$	95.42	57.69	.000
Social	3.78$_a$	3.92$_a$	3.96$_a$	2.07	2.47	.086
Personal/ medical	3.42$_a$	3.36$_a$	3.65$_a$	1.98	2.21	.111

Notes: Higher mean scores reflect greater agreement with QDIO items. For example, young adults self-report higher levels of disability pride and lower levels of exclusion. Type III Sum of Squares (Type III SS), F-values, and significance levels were obtained from a multiple analysis of variance (MANOVA). Means in the same row that do not share subscripts differ at $p < .05$.

We also conducted ordinary least squares (OLS) multiple regression analyses by regressing each of the four factors—pride, exclusion, social model, and medical model—on age, marital status, employment status, race, gender, size of community, educational level, whether the respondent had a mobility-related disability, length of time with a disability, level of assistance required with activities of daily living, level of social activity, and level of activism. Results are shown in Table 8.3. Despite the relatively small sample size (n = 388), removing nonsignificant predictors did not affect the results.

Age was a significant predictor of level of disability pride. Middle-aged respondents had a significantly lower level of disability pride than young adults, as did older respondents. Other significant predictors of disability pride were race, work status, community size, length of time with disability, level of assistance required, and level of activism. Non–European Americans demonstrated lower levels of disability pride than European Americans, as did respondents from smaller towns and rural areas. Respondents who had been disabled longer displayed higher levels of pride, as did respondents who required less assistance with activities of daily living. The strongest predictor of pride was level of activism: respondents with lower levels of activism or with no activism had the lowest level of disability pride. The overall model was statistically significant and had an explained variance of 22 percent.

With regard to exclusion, age was again a significant predictor. Middle-aged respondents reported significantly greater levels of exclusion than young adults. Older respondents also felt more excluded than young respondents, although the difference was not as great as it was for middle-aged respondents and was not statistically significant.

Table 8.3 OLS Regressions for the Four Disability Factors (*N* = 388)

Independent Variable	EQ 1 Pride		EQ 2 Exclusion		EQ 3 Social		EQ 4 Medical	
	b	Beta	*b*	Beta	*b*	Beta	*b*	Beta
Age								
18–35 years	—	—	—	—	—	—	—	—
36–64 years	−.46[a]	−.22	.46[b]	.21	−.02	−.01	.01	.004
65 and over	−.69[a]	−.17	.23	.05	.17	.06	.06	.02
Nonwhite (binary)	−.25[a]	−.09	−.03	−.01	−.02	−.01	.11	.06
Level of education								
(ordinal)	.05	.07	−.05	−.06	.002	.01	−.03	−.05
Employment status								
Student	—	—	—	—	—	—	—	—
Work full-time								
or part-time	.26[a]	.10	−.24[a]	−.09	−.01	−.01	−.02	−.01
Retired	.36	.12	.40[a]	.13	−.04	−.02	.26[a]	.12
Unemployed or								
homemaker	.24	.09	.33[b]	.13	.02	.01	.03	.02
Respondent is female								
(binary)	−.04	−.02	−.16[a]	−.08	.09	.07	−.12[a]	−.09
Marital status								
Never married	—	—	—	—	—	—	—	—
Married	−.04	−.02	−.14	−.06	−.06	−.04	−.22[a]	−.13
Separated, widowed,								
or divorced	−.11	−.04	.40[b]	.15	.12	.07	.05	.03
Size of community								
lived in (ordinal)	−.11[b]	−.14	−.05	−.06	−.03	−.06	.06[a]	.11
Disability status and activity								
Rs has mobility								
disability (binary)	−.11	−.05	.12	.06	.16[a]	.13	−.13	−.09
Length of time with								
disability (ordinal)	.13[b]	.17	−.05	−.07	.01	.03	−.03	−.06
Level of assistance								
required (ordinal)	.18[a]	.12	−.27[b]	−.18	−.08	−.08	−.05	−.05
Social activities outside								
home (ordinal)	−.04	−.04	.26[b]	.25	−.05	−.09	.07[a]	.10
Level of activism	−.19[b]	−.21	.03	.03	−.11[b]	−.19	.12[b]	.20
R-Square	.22[b]		.45[b]		.11[b]		.14[b]	

Notes: a. *p* < .05 (1-tailed)

　b. *p* <.01 (1-tailed)

　b refers to unstandardized regression coefficient; Beta refers to standardized regression coefficient. High mean scores on the factors represent higher levels of disability pride, feelings of exclusion, agreement with the social model, and agreement with the personal/medical model.

A strong predictor of exclusion was employment status, with retired respondents indicating significantly greater feelings of exclusion than students. In addition, respondents who were unemployed or were homemakers had significantly greater feelings of exclusion than students. Respondents who were employed either full-time or part-time reported the least amount of exclusion. Separated, widowed, and divorced survey participants reported greater feelings of exclusion than never-married respondents. Participants who required more assistance with activities of daily living and who reported lower levels of social activities also demonstrated greater levels of exclusion. The overall model for exclusion was quite robust, with an explained variance of 45 percent.

Age was not a significant predictor of the social model subscale. Only two predictors were statistically significant. Respondents with a mobility impairment reported a greater level of adherence to a social model, as did respondents with higher levels of activism. The overall model was statistically significant, although only 11 percent of the variance in the social factor was explained by the model.

Age was also not a significant predictor of the medical factor. There were six statistically significant predictors, and the explained variance was 14 percent. Retired respondents, male respondents, and respondents who reported fewer social activities and less activism were all more likely to report higher levels of agreement with the medical model. Finally, married participants reported lower levels of agreement with the medical model.

Discussion

Not surprisingly, older people appear to be less likely to adopt newer views such as the social model and disability pride. Stigma and the medical model have been the normative views of disability for many years, and older individuals are likely to have been socialized to adhere to these views. As our data suggest, they also are less likely than younger people to use e-mail or the Internet, often the primary means of disseminating the social model.

Older individuals also had the most significant disabilities of any age group, and most had acquired their disabilities later in life. Perhaps they were too involved in issues of rehabilitation or coping to engage in activism. As noted in Chapter 7, activism is time-consuming and requires at least a minimal level of energy that is less likely to exist among older people, even those without significant disabilities. Further, lack of exposure to the Internet, which has become an important organizing tool, could explain lack of activism as well as a lack of exposure to the social model in general. The relative lack of activism among the youngest members of the sample is perhaps better explained by the apathy among the young toward political activism in general that has been reported elsewhere in the literature.

Age is associated with length of time with disability, and members of the youngest age group in our sample typically had their disabilities since birth. In the oldest age group, however, disabilities were likely to have been recently acquired. As reported in the last chapter, we found that the primary determinant of positive disability identity seems to be whether or not one is born with a disability, a finding also reported by H. D. Hahn and T. L. Belt (2004). This finding suggests a significant limitation on the interpretation of our results. Because of the association in our sample between age and age at disability onset, we cannot know which of these variables accounts for the age-related associations we have found. People with lifelong disabilities learn from an early age to feel comfortable with their identity, whereas those who acquire disabilities later in life have already been socialized into the societal norm of stigma, probably resulting in a lack of disability pride. Further research is needed to determine the true effect of age alone.

Not surprisingly, older respondents reported lower levels of social participation and life satisfaction than younger ones. As the data showed, younger respondents are more likely than older respondents to have friends with disabilities, perhaps encouraging a view that disability is normative. This finding is interesting because disability increases with age. Perhaps older respondents continue to define their status in relation to a nondisabled reference group rather than to their more disabled peers, resulting in lowered self-esteem and greater feelings of exclusion. Because life satisfaction is generally a desired outcome, an understanding of the factors involved in reduced satisfaction among older people with disabilities could be valuable in the design of intervention programs for this population.

Clearly, further research is needed to establish the accuracy of the explanations offered here. Our convenience sample was limited in size and was not representative of the US population as a whole, nor of populations in other countries. In particular, younger people were overrepresented in the sample in comparison with their numbers among people with disabilities in the general population. In addition, the association we found between age and age at disability onset points to a need for further research with a sample that is large and diverse enough to control for age at onset. Also, although somewhat representative geographically, our sample was not drawn randomly from the US population.

Qualitative studies are needed as well to substantiate our assumptions about the direction of effects. We assume that age is an independent variable that determines identity, model, and activism. However, other factors may serve as mediating variables, and future research should explore the processes through which people come to adopt various orientations toward disability and how these orientations change over time in relation to the presence or absence of various interactional opportunities. Increased knowledge about the career paths of individuals with disabilities would be valuable for practitioners and policymakers in their work to increase opportunities for this population.

Our findings suggest that age is negatively associated with life satisfaction. In other analyses of these data, we found that life satisfaction appears to be associated with disability orientation, apart from age. In general, individuals with an affirmative activism or a typicality orientation seemed to have greater life satisfaction than those with other orientations. Perhaps then, older individuals need to be exposed to newer perspectives on disability such as the social model in order to increase their perceived quality of life.

Conclusion: Age and Disability Orientation

Although the literature on the self-views of young people with disabilities is generally qualitative, it clearly suggests that this population tends to view disability as something natural. Many children and young adults with congenital disabilities do not seem to have internalized societal stigma, possibly because their significant others have provided alternative, positive definitions of them. Although some of these individuals appear to have embraced an orientation of affirmative typicality, their affirmation is not based in the social model. Instead, they seem to want to "fit in" with their nondisabled peers. Activism may occur later after an encounter with the disability rights movement. However, many who have the opportunity to work and to engage in the ordinary activities of daily life choose to maintain a typicality orientation throughout their lives.

Disabilities acquired later in life appear to be more likely to have a negative impact on the self-esteem of those who acquire them. Most people in society have been exposed to stigma and the medical model and have learned to view disability negatively as a result. Both the qualitative and quantitative literature suggests that older people with newly acquired disabilities will have a personal activism or resignation orientation, unless they have the resources to continue to participate in their prior employment and social activities. With time, some of these individuals may adopt a typicality or affirmative activism orientation, depending on their opportunity structures. Those who acquire their disabilities in young adulthood or middle age appear somewhat more likely than those who are older to become involved in disability rights activism. The elderly appear to more commonly adopt a resignation orientation upon becoming disabled, perhaps, in part, because they have not been exposed to the social model. In general, those who acquire disabilities late in life appear to view their disabilities less positively than those who are born with them.

Note

The material in the section "An Empirical Study of Age and Disability Orientation" is based largely on Rosalyn Benjamin Darling and D. Alex Heckert, "Orientations Toward Disability: Differences over the Lifecourse," *International Journal of Disability, Development and Education* 57, no. 2): 131–144.

9

Disability and Identity: Past, Present, and Future

In this book, a work of sociology, I have focused on the role that interaction in society plays in shaping the way people with disabilities view themselves and their disabilities. Clearly, factors other than social interaction contribute to the self-views of individuals, and much has been written about the impact of impairments themselves—their associated pain or inconvenience—on the way people view their disabilities. Recent literature in disability studies is replete with studies that look at the relationship between body and self. However, medical sociology has a long, empirically-based tradition of studying social structure and social interaction as powerful shapers of the way individuals react to illness and disability. People with identical impairments may view their situation very differently if they have different ethnic backgrounds or different experiences. Thus, although I do not deny the role of the body, I have taken the position throughout this book that understanding social reactions to disability is an important, and perhaps the most important, factor in understanding disability identity and orientation.

Society has changed since Erving Goffman wrote about "spoiled identity" in 1963. The growth of the disability rights movement and other social changes have resulted in newer, more positive views of people with disabilities. Although stigma has certainly not disappeared, its nature and effects are different from those that prevailed fifty years ago. This book has attempted to address the question of how these changes might have influenced the identities and orientations toward disability of those affected. In the following sections, I

141

review the conclusions from the previous chapters about the likely effects of stigma and its changes. Then I will speculate about how disability identity and orientation may change in the future and propose an agenda for research.

Stigma and Acceptance: Societal Views of Disability

As I explained in Chapter 2, the prevailing view of disability in Western society until late in the twentieth century was one of stigma. Goffman and others used terms like *tainted* and *discounted* to describe the way people with disabilities were viewed by others in society. Until fairly recently, many people with disabilities were hidden from public view in institutions or at home, and those who ventured out in public commonly engaged in passing or covering to avoid calling attention to their "discreditable" attributes. Stigma was not uniformly applied to different individuals or disabilities, however, and research suggests some variation relating to the nature of the disability and other variables.

These negative views were reflected in the media. Movies, television, and other media portrayed people with disabilities in stereotypical terms, such as pitiable or evil, and such portrayals, in turn, reinforced the views of their audience. The media tended to promote the medical model of disability, in which disability was regarded as an individual problem rather than a social construction.

Although stigma appears to be a universal phenomenon, some variability exists in how disability is viewed in various cultural and subcultural groups. Some cultures have practiced infanticide against children born with disabilities, whereas other cultures have celebrated disability associated with heroism in war or other valued behaviors. Even Americans do not hold monolithic views toward disability. Research has shown that racial and ethnic background and socioeconomic status play a role in shaping disability-related attitudes. Yet all groups seem to have attached stigma to at least some disabilities at one time or another.

Since the late 1970s, a growing body of literature has documented the emergence of more positive views. The ascendance of the disability rights movement and its attendant social model of disability have resulted in increasing acceptance of people with disabilities in many areas of life. Today, in advertisements and on television, disabled individuals sometimes appear alongside their nondisabled counterparts playing ordinary roles. Yet evidence of stigma continues to exist in indicators such as the high rate of unemployment among people with disabilities and high rates of abuse and hate crimes against disabled individuals.

Have Society's Views Been Internalized?

People with disabilities continue to be exposed to stigma along with more positive views. Labeling theory in sociology contends that, as a result of their interactions in society, these people will internalize the negative views of others and incorporate them into their self-concepts. Early studies by psychologists and psychiatrists seemed to support this contention by finding low levels of self-esteem and high levels of maladjustment in their disabled subjects. However, many of these studies used flawed methodologies that produced the results the investigators had anticipated. More recent studies have mostly found that, with a few notable exceptions, self-esteem does not differ significantly between disabled and nondisabled samples. These findings raise questions about the validity of labeling theory and the looking-glass self theory on which it is based.

These questions may be addressed by other concepts from symbolic interaction theory that can explain the apparent discrepancy between societal views and the self-views of individuals. Societal views are filtered through interactions with reference groups and significant others. Although some parents seem to transmit negative attitudes toward disability to their children, others, especially those who do not have strong, preconceived notions of what their children will be like, seem to accept their children's limitations and to foster high self-esteem. Even individuals who leave childhood with negative self-conceptions often encounter turning points later in life, at which new significant others evaluate them positively. Self-concept development and identity formation are ongoing processes that continue throughout the life course as individuals encounter new situations and new definitions from significant others.

In social interaction, individuals choose how to present themselves. Self-presentation is situational, and people with disabilities may downplay their disabilities or try to pass in some situations and yet proudly reveal their disabilities in others. Such choices reflect the significance of the others present in the situation, the perceived attitudes toward disability of those others, and the importance of the situation for the individual.

Moreover, people with disabilities have self-concepts that include many identities, not just disability identity. In many cases, these other identities are more salient than the one associated with the disability. The salience of disability identity is likely to increase when *society* calls it to someone's attention through stigma or discrimination.

Multiple Devalued Identities

As just noted, disability identity is but one of a constellation of identities within the self-concept of a person with a disability. In some cases, disability might be the person's most salient identity; in others, disability may be a minor or even nonexistent part of his or her self-concept.

A number of researchers have looked at the interactions between multiple devalued identities within a single individual. Although identity salience is situational, disability identity may be overshadowed by race, gender, or other identities, depending on a number of variables. Some disability rights activists have expressed concern that the movement would be weakened by the inclusion of race or gender issues, suggesting a need to choose one identity over another. Other writers have looked at the nature of the relationship between identities, using terms like *double discrimination* and *simultaneous oppression.*

Disabled women are faced with sometimes unattainable cultural role prescriptions like physical attractiveness, sexuality, and caregiving. Studies suggest that a large number of women have internalized these prescriptions and have low self-esteem, probably as a result. In general, disabled women tend to experience more discrimination and to have lower self-esteem than disabled men. Yet many examples exist of women with disabilities who have managed to view themselves positively. Positive self-definitions often result from interaction with members of the disability rights movement, who promote a social model and disability pride.

Studies of the identity of African Americans with disabilities have had a theme of simultaneous oppression. They have also noted that these individuals are often doubly isolated because they are rejected by both the African American and the disability communities.

For some, their racial and disability identities are inseparable. Yet a number of writers have argued that racial identity tends to be more salient than disability identity in American society. Chapter 4 presented a typology of identities in relation to both disability pride and black pride.

Identity Politics and Disability Pride

In Chapters 2, 3, and 4, I explored stigma and its likely effects on self-concept. In Chapter 5, I shifted focus to a societal movement away from stigma and the medical model of disability and toward the identity of disability pride that the movement promoted. The disability rights movement of the 1970s and 1980s grew out of earlier social movements by other disadvantaged groups, new opportunities for networking, and improved technology. The principles of the movement included the reframing of disability as a social and political problem and the quest for individual and collective empowerment and self-determination.

On an individual level, the movement fostered the self-worth of individuals with disabilities, claiming or affirmation of disability as a positive status, and recognition that people with disabilities belonged to a cultural minority group. Although the value of identity politics has been challenged by some, the proportion of people with disabilities who share a sense of common identity with people like themselves has been increasing in recent years. Some psychologists have argued that coming out as a person with a disability is a last step in the path toward a positive disability identity.

In Chapter 5, I presented a sociological model of disability identity development. Most people who become activists have experienced stigma and/or possess a strong sense of justice. However, movement membership is typically contingent on a turning point in the form of an encounter with one or more individuals who are already members. Potential members commonly form emotional bonds with these individuals and later come to adopt the views of their new significant others. The process is completed through identity work that includes mechanisms such as hearing narratives and practicing rituals that confirm that one's oppression is shared. Disability identities other than pride develop in similar ways—through interaction with significant others. Disability pride and activism seem most common among individuals with visible disabilities.

Diversity of Identity and Orientation Toward Disability

Although pride and activism appear to be increasing, they still seem to characterize a minority of the population of people with disabilities in society today. In Chapter 6, I presented a literature-based typology of orientations toward disability, including typicality, personal activism, affirmative activism, resignation, apathy, isolated affirmative activism, and situational identification. These types are based on access to opportunities for integration into either mainstream society or the disability rights movement and disability culture. Like all ideal types, they represent polar positions, and, although actual individuals may tend toward one type or another, they are unlikely to be perfect examples of any one type.

In keeping with the model presented in Chapter 5, these types are not static; they are subject to change as individuals move through orientation careers. Thus, people who see themselves as victims with no hope for relief (resignation) may move to an orientation of typicality after encountering a helpful rehabilitation professional or to an orientation of affirmative activism after meeting a member of the disability rights movement. Although the literature supports the existence of these diverse outcomes, population-based empirical research is needed to determine the actual proportion of people who approximate each type.

A Study Based on the Operationalization of the Typology

Based on both the literature described above and interviews with people with disabilities, I developed the Questionnaire on Disability, Identity, and Opportunity to measure both the components of disability orientation (identity, model, and role) and access to opportunities for integration into mainstream society and into the disability subculture. The instrument was tested with a national convenience sample of people with disabilities, and the results supported the typology presented in Chapter 6.

Cluster analysis produced five types: affirmative typicality, normative typicality, personal activism, affirmative activism, and resignation. Those in the typicality clusters tended to be younger and less disabled and to have high levels of inclusion in mainstream society.

They did not participate in disability rights activism or other aspects of disability culture. Those in the affirmative typicality cluster tended to have their disabilities from birth and to have some disability pride, whereas those in the normative typicality cluster tended to have acquired disabilities and to reject disability pride. Those in the affirmative activism cluster had high levels of inclusion in mainstream society as well, but they also participated in disability-related organizations and disability rights activism. They had high levels of disability pride and tended to have had their disabilities since birth. Those in the personal activism cluster tended to be excluded from mainstream society and to engage in disability-related activism. Most had their disabilities since birth and had some disability pride. Finally, those in the resignation cluster tended to be older and to have acquired disabilities. They were likely to be excluded from mainstream society but did not engage in activism, and they rejected disability pride.

These findings confirm the existence of a diversity of orientations toward disability and support several literature-based conclusions. As expected, activism tends to be associated with disability pride. However, a positive view of one's disability seems to be most strongly associated with time of disability acquisition: people with lifelong disabilities tend to have higher levels of pride than those who have acquired their disabilities later in life. Exclusion from mainstream society seems to be an impetus to activism for some (the personal activists), but other activists (the affirmative activists) seem to be motivated by strong ties to the disability rights movement. As the literature suggests, these individuals are likely to view their fellow activists as a reference group that affirms their self-esteem. The most common orientation in this sample was typicality. Those with less disabling conditions who are able to participate in mainstream society seem to avoid associating with disability-related organizations, whether or not they reject an identity of disability pride.

Because this study did not use a probability sample, we still have no way of knowing the proportion of people in the larger population of people with disabilities who approximate each type. In particular, the orientations of people who are not associated with disability organizations of any kind are not known; at least some probably do not even identify as people with disabilities. In addition, the size of the sample used in this study did not allow for analyses that controlled for some important factors. Further research is especially needed to clarify the relationship between age and age at disability acquisition. The study, which was conducted in the mid-2000s, suggests that stigma still plays a role in the identity choices made by people with disabilities in the United States. Those with the highest levels of life satisfaction appear to be the individuals who are able to overcome stigma through their acceptance in mainstream society or through the support they receive from the disability subculture.

Timing

The study described above was a cross-sectional one. The results reflect the orientations of people at a single point in time. Yet as I've argued throughout this book, identities and orientations are likely to change over the life course. Studies of children with disabilities seem to suggest that most have positive self-concepts. Yet many engage in a process of negotiating a "normalized" identity, especially in interactions with nondisabled friends. Awareness of disability rights activism and an affirmation orientation appear to be lacking in this population.

As these children age, they are likely to try to maintain a typicality orientation. However, experiences with stigma and encounters with activists may lead them in a different direction. Although longitudinal studies of people with lifelong disabilities are lacking, some people who age with disability seem to maintain their self-esteem through interactions within friendship groups of others like themselves; deaf people typify this adaptation. Those with later onset disabilities, however, tend to view the acquisition of a devalued identity as a crisis. Further analysis of the data used to validate the QDIO showed that older people, who have generally acquired their disabilities later in life, are more likely to feel excluded from social participation and to reject an identity of disability pride. They also have lower levels of life satisfaction than younger people and those disabled from birth.

Identity Change and Career Paths

In several places in this book, I have questioned whether the identities of people with disabilities have changed since the publication of Goffman's *Stigma* in 1963. In strictly empirical terms, the question is unanswerable. In 1963, no one conducted studies of disability identity and orientation similar to the recent ones being discussed here. There is considerable evidence that societal attitudes toward disability have evolved over time, but conclusions about whether these attitude shifts are reflected in the self-concepts of individuals with disabilities must rely on theoretical arguments about the relationship between society and the individual.

But recent studies show that we do know something about current self-views in this population. Perhaps the most significant conclusion to be drawn from the information I have presented in this book is that these self-views are diverse. Current orientations toward disability include some that did not appear in the literature fifty years ago (e.g., affirmative activism), along with sigma-based views that are similar to those reported by Goffman.

Thus, orientations toward disability appear to have become more diverse since Goffman's time. Although many individuals continue to experience stigma and oppression, some have been able to reject society's negative evaluations through their association with members of the disability rights movement or through access to opportunities for acceptance in mainstream society. Identities of disabled individuals today range from negative self-views to disability pride. Figure 9.1 depicts some common career paths leading to the orientations discussed above. Not all career paths are linear, and some individuals move back and forth between orientations as they encounter new turning points in life. Figure 9.1 shows what appear to be the most common career paths based on the research reported in this book.

The primary determinants of identity seem to be timing and opportunities. Those with lifelong disabilities appear to have more positive self-views than those who acquire their disabilities later in life. In addition, two types of opportunity seem to play a role in promoting high self-esteem and life satisfaction in this population: (1) acceptance in mainstream society (generally more available to those with less visible and/or functionally less significant impairments) and (2) encounters with representatives of a disability subculture, including the disability rights movement. Conversely, individuals who are isolated by age, race, poverty, or other barriers to these opportunities tend to have more negative identities and less life satisfaction.

These findings suggest several initiatives for policy and practice:

1. On a macrolevel, policymakers need to continue to promote legislation that breaks down physical and social barriers to full

Figure 9.1 Common Careers of Disability Orientation

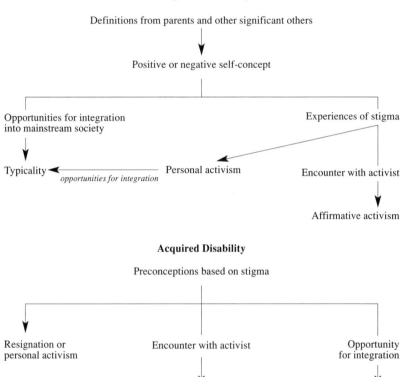

inclusion for people with disabilities. In addition, those charged with enforcing existing legislation like the Americans with Disabilities Act need to ensure compliance on a wider scale.

2. On a microlevel, practitioners need to create opportunities for interaction between their clients with disabilities and representatives of the disability culture and disability rights communities.

3. Individuals with disabilities themselves need to find ways to connect with opportunities that already exist and work to increase the opportunities available in their communities.

What Lies Ahead?

Future changes in disability identity will depend to a large extent on the implementation of the policy and practice initiatives listed in the last section, "Identity Change and Career Paths." However, some trends, both favorable and unfavorable for positive identity development, are suggested by recent events in neonatal decisionmaking.

In the 1970s, the celebrated Baby Doe case and others showcased the negative attitudes toward persons with disabilities that prevailed at the time. These cases were based on decisions by physicians and parents to deny life-saving treatment to newborns with disabilities because life with disability was believed to lack quality. At the time, many disability organizations protested these decisions, and legislation and court decisions led to the treatment of most disabled newborns (Darling 2008).

Technological advances now enable many parents to decide, even before birth, to terminate a pregnancy in which the child has a disability. Although stigma is declining to some extent in modern society, most parents choose to terminate such pregnancies. One study (Mansfield et al. 1999) found that prenatal diagnosis results in pregnancy termination 92 percent of the time in the case of Down syndrome and 64 percent of the time in the case of spina bifida, two of the most common impairments diagnosed prenatally.

Because many disabilities are not diagnosed until after birth, parents and physicians continue to make treatment decisions in the case of newborns with impairments of various kinds. A small number of these recent decisions seem to reflect the influence of the disability rights movement. In the mid-2000s, a case in Great Britain that received a considerable amount of Internet attention involved the parents of a child named Charlotte, who fought to reverse a "do not resuscitate" order, arguing that Charlotte's life had as much value as that of a person without disabilities. However, numerous other Internet accounts suggest that, more commonly, parents and physicians jointly decide to remove life support from infants with impairments involving "brain damage" (Darling 2008).

Although recent research is lacking, some early studies (Holt 1958; Mercer 1965; Seligman and Darling 2007) suggest that upper-SES parents are less accepting of children with disabilities than those of lower status. B. Khoshnood and colleagues (2006) report lower rates of prenatal diagnosis and pregnancy termination among lower-SES parents than among those of higher status but suggest that both access issues and preferences may contribute to this finding. At least some well-educated parents have embraced the parenting of children with major disabilities. For example, G. H. Landsman (1998) describes her life with a child with significant impairments in positive terms, and M. Berube (1996) writes about the joys of living with a child with Down syndrome. Like those with an affirmative activism orientation, these well-educated parents have been exposed to the tenets of the disability rights movement. However, other highly educated parents (see, e.g., Alecson 1995) have come to view children as "perfectible commodities" and have opted not to treat infants whose disabilities would prevent them from leading the lives their parents had envisioned.

Because disability continues to be viewed negatively by many in society, increased availability of technological advances in prenatal diagnosis probably will result in fewer infants being born with disabilities, regardless of the message of the disability rights movement. Thus, the segment of the disabled population most likely to have positive disability identities—namely, those disabled from birth—will probably decrease. The challenge for the future, then, may be the reframing of identity construction among those with disabilities acquired later in life—a population that is increasing.

A Research Agenda

To date, no large-scale, population-based studies of disability identity exist. Consequently, this book has relied on studies based on smaller, nonrepresentative samples and personal and anecdotal accounts by people with disabilities. Virtually all these studies have obtained their respondents through disability-related organizations of various kinds. As a result, we should be hesitant to generalize their findings to the larger population of people with disabilities in Western society today. In particular, two groups of people with disabilities have been largely excluded: (1) those who have no association with disability-related organizations and who may not even identify as disabled and (2) isolated individuals with significant disabilities, including intellectual disabilities, who do not participate in disability-related organizations. Thus, the typicality and resignation categories described in earlier chapters are probably underrepresented in the literature. In addition, more research with understudied minorities, such as African Americans and gays and lesbians with disabilities, is needed. Instruments like the QDIO need to be administered to randomly selected, popula-tion-based samples to better map the existing range of orientations toward disability.

In addition, instruments that measure salience of disability iden-tity need to be developed. The Twenty Statements Test (Kuhn and McPartland 1954) might be able to be adapted for this purpose, or newer measures might be needed. The findings from existing studies suggest several hypotheses relating to salience:

1. Disability identity will be most salient for individuals with an affirmative activism orientation toward disability and least salient for individuals with a typicality orientation.
2. Disability identity will be more salient among individuals with visible disabilities than among those with invisible disabilities.
3. Disability identity will be more salient than racial or gender identity among white men but less salient than racial or gender identity among African Americans or women.
4. Disability identity will be more salient among individuals who have experienced stigma or discrimination than among those who have been accepted in mainstream society.

Further research is needed as well to link quality of life with dis-ability orientation. Although both affirmative activism and typicality appear to be associated with life satisfaction, instruments such as the Comprehensive Quality of Life Scale (Cummins 2012) or the Per-ceived Quality of Life Scale (Patrick 2012) could be administered along with the QDIO to further establish and clarify the association between orientation and perceived life quality. Orientations linked with high quality of life could then be fostered through policy and practice initiatives.

Although cross-sectional, quantitative research can shed light on the nature and correlates of disability identity in the population of people with disabilities, it cannot explain the processes through which identities and orientations are acquired. Thus, the link between societal attitudes and the self-views of individuals remains only a hy-pothesis (albeit one supported by the existing qualitative literature). Further qualitative research and longitudinal studies are needed to elucidate these processes. Ideally, a large-scale study would follow a cohort of individuals over time. The sample would include individu-als disabled from birth along with nondisabled young people who may acquire disabilities as they age. The respondents would periodically report disability status and complete instruments measuring disability identity, orientation, and quality of life.

On a smaller scale, qualitative studies could look further at the career paths of individuals with lifelong and acquired disabilities. Depth interviews would reveal the interactional histories of these individuals and determine the turning points at which changes in identity occurred. The types of significant others most influential in shaping identity could also be determined. The findings of such studies would contribute to our knowledge of role and identity development and would have practical applications in designing interventions to promote positive interactional experiences.

Conclusion

Although I intended that this book would update the conclusions of Goffman's classic study of stigma and "spoiled identity," it has not completely achieved its intention. Much has been written about stigma and self-concept over the years, but empirical evidence remains limited in scope. This book provides a kind of meta-analysis based on the present state of our knowledge, and the findings presented here increase our understanding in important ways that I reiterate below.

One major contribution of this volume is the application of a sociological version of identity theory to explain disability identity development. Identity theory has expanded since the time of Goffman's writing. His work was based on the premise of symbolic interaction theory that individuals act in response to the self-definitions they receive from others. The theory has since been refined to explain the variability in individuals' responses. We know that some definitions are more influential than others and that some interactions serve as buffers to prevent the internalization of negative appraisals.

An understanding of the relation between interactional processes and self-concept development produces a more nuanced view than the one guiding Goffman's study. Another contribution of this book is its focus on diversity within the disability community. A review of the literature and a recent study revealed several orientations toward disability and a range of identities—some "spoiled" and some not. The book also explored some of the factors associated with this variation, including timing and opportunity structures, which had not previously received much attention in the literature.

Yet much of Goffman's contribution remains important. Certainly, as this book has shown, stigma has not disappeared; rather, it continues to be a potent force in the shaping of identity among many, or even most, individuals with disabilities in modern society. Even identities like disability pride, which reject stigma, appear to have developed as a direct response to it. The major change in disability identity over the past fifty years appears to be one of increasing diversity. Although in the past most people with disabilities seem to have seen themselves through the lens of stigma, today people have more identity options that, we can hope, will continue to increase in the future. So much of our discourse on disability and identity in the past fifty years has been colored by Goffman's seminal work. My intention in writing this book was to continue that conversation.

Appendix

Questionnaire on Disability Identity and Opportunity

Please read each of the following statements and check (√) the box that best represents your level of agreement:	Strongly Agree	Agree	Not Sure	Disagree	Strongly Disagree
1. I don't think of myself as a disabled person.	☐	☐	☐	☐	☐
2. I would rather associate with disabled people than with people without disabilities.	☐	☐	☐	☐	☐
3. I am a better person because of my disability.	☐	☐	☐	☐	☐
4. If I had a choice, I would prefer not to have a disability.	☐	☐	☐	☐	☐
5. I am proud of my disability.	☐	☐	☐	☐	☐
6. My disability is an important part of who I am.	☐	☐	☐	☐	☐
7. I feel sorry for people with disabilities.	☐	☐	☐	☐	☐
8. Most of my friends have disabilities.	☐	☐	☐	☐	☐
9. Lack of accessibility and discrimination by employers are the main reasons why disabled people are unemployed.	☐	☐	☐	☐	☐
10. It isn't easy for people with disabilities to be treated as "normal."	☐	☐	☐	☐	☐
11. People with disabilities need to fight for their rights more than nondisabled people do.	☐	☐	☐	☐	☐
12. The reason most people with disabilities are unemployed is that they are not able to do the jobs that are available.	☐	☐	☐	☐	☐
13. My disability limits my social life.	☐	☐	☐	☐	☐
14. My disability keeps me from working.	☐	☐	☐	☐	☐
15. The biggest problem faced by people with disabilities is the attitudes of other people.	☐	☐	☐	☐	☐

2

		Strongly Agree	Agree	Not Sure	Disagree	Strongly Disagree
16.	All buildings should be accessible to people with disabilities.	☐	☐	☐	☐	☐
17.	I have a lot in common with other people with disabilities.	☐	☐	☐	☐	☐
18.	I wish that someone would find a cure for my disability.	☐	☐	☐	☐	☐
19.	Doctors and other medical professionals know what is best for people with disabilities.	☐	☐	☐	☐	☐
20.	People with disabilities need to learn to adjust to living in a world in which most people are not disabled.	☐	☐	☐	☐	☐
21.	I try to hide my disability whenever I can.	☐	☐	☐	☐	☐
22.	I am familiar with the Americans with Disabilities Act (ADA) and think it is a good law.	☐	☐	☐	☐	☐
23.	I am familiar with the Disability Rights Movement and support its goals.	☐	☐	☐	☐	☐
24.	People should try to overcome their disabilities.	☐	☐	☐	☐	☐
25.	My disability enriches my life.	☐	☐	☐	☐	☐
26.	People with disabilities can never fit into "normal" society.	☐	☐	☐	☐	☐
27.	In general, I am satisfied with the quality of my life.	☐	☐	☐	☐	☐
28.	I often am excluded from activities because of my disability.	☐	☐	☐	☐	☐
29.	The people I care about always include me in activities I am able to enjoy.	☐	☐	☐	☐	☐
30.	The most important thing for people with disabilities is to learn to accept what they cannot change.	☐	☐	☐	☐	☐

3

Please answer the following questions by placing a check (√) next to the description that applies to you:

1. What is your gender?

☐ Male   ☐ Female

2. What is your age?

☐ 18 – 35   ☐ 36 – 64   ☐ Over 65

3. What is your marital status?

☐ Never married   ☐ Married   ☐ Separated   ☐ Widowed
                                    or divorced

4. What is your employment status?

☐ Work full-time   ☐ Work part-time   ☐ Retired

☐ Unemployed or homemaker   ☐ Student

5. Where do you live?

☐ Small town   ☐ Rural area   ☐ Large City

☐ Medium-sized or small city

☐ Suburb of a large or medium-sized city

6. What is the highest level of school you completed?

☐ Less than high school   ☐ High school

☐ Some college   ☐ College

☐ Some graduate school   ☐ Graduate school

4

7. What is the nature of your disability, handicap, or impairment? (If you have more than one, please check as many as apply.)

☐ Mobility (Difficulty in movement)

☐ Vision

☐ Hearing

☐ Speech

☐ Cognitive (Difficulty in thinking)

☐ Cosmetic (Difference in appearance or size)

☐ Other: Please specify: _____

8. How long have you had your disability, handicap, or impairment (If you have more than one, please check the time that describes the condition you have had the *longest*.)

☐ Since birth   ☐ More than 10 years

☐ 5 – 10 years   ☐ Less than 5 years

9. How much assistance do you need with activities of daily living (like bathing, dressing, shopping, and cooking)?

☐ I need assistance with all activities.

☐ I need assistance with some activities.

☐ I don't need any assistance.

5

10. About how often do you engage in social activities outside of your home, like visiting friends or eating out in restaurants?

   ☐ More than once a week

   ☐ Once or several times a month

   ☐ Occasionally, less than once a month

   ☐ Rarely or never

11. Have you ever participated in a demonstration, written a letter to your congressional representative, or engaged in another activity to try to increase the opportunities available to people with disabilities?

   ☐ Yes, many times   ☐ Yes, a few times   ☐ Yes, once

   ☐ No, never

12. Please check the activities in which you participate at least once a month:

   ☐ Talking on the telephone with family, friends, or acquaintances

   ☐ Using a computer to communicate by e-mail

   ☐ Using a computer to access disability-related websites on the Internet

   ☐ Using a computer to access other websites

   ☐ Going to meetings or other activities sponsored by disability-related organizations

   ☐ Going to meetings or activities of other organizations

   ☐ Attending religious services

   ☐ Reading magazines or newsletters from disability-related organizations

6

13. Please check the category that best describes your total, annual
household income:

☐ Under $25,000   ☐ $25,000 - $50,000

☐ $50,000 - $100,000   ☐ Over $100,000

14. Please check the category or categories that best describe your
racial/ethnic background:

☐ European American (white)

☐ African American

☐ Latino or Hispanic

☐ Native American or Indian

☐ Asian American

☐ Other: _____

THANK YOU!

References

Albrecht, G. L., et al. (1982). "Social distance from the stigmatized." *Social Science and Medicine* 16(14): 1319–1327.

Alcoff, L. M., and S. P. Mohanty (2006). Reconsidering identity politics: An introduction. *Identity Politics Reconsidered*, ed. L. M. Alcoff, M. Hames-Garcia, S. P. Mohanty, and P. M. I. Moya. New York: Palgrave Macmillan, 1–9.

Alecson, D. G. (1995). *Lost Lullaby*. Berkeley: University of California Press.

Alston, R. J., et al. (1996). "Racial identity and African Americans with disabilities: Theoretical and practical considerations." *Journal of Rehabilitation* 62: 11–15.

Anspach, R. R. (1979). "From stigma to identity politics: Political activism among the physically disabled and former mental patients." *Social Science and Medicine* 13A: 765–773.

Antie, B. J. (2004). "Factors associated with self-worth in young people with physical disabilities." *Health and Social Work* 29(3): 167–175.

Asch, A. (1984). "Personal reflections." *American Psychologist* 39(5): 551–552.

——— (2004). "Critical race theory, feminism, and disability." *Gendering Disability*, ed. B. G. Smith and B. Hutchison. New Brunswick, NJ: Rutgers University Press, 9–44.

Avery, D. M. (1999). Talking "tragedy": Identity issues in the parental story of disability. *Disability Discourse*, ed. M. Corker and S. French. Buckingham, Open University Press.

Baca Zinn, M. P., and Angela Y. H. Pok (2002). Tradition and transition in Mexican-origin families. *Minority Families in the United States: A Multicultural Perspective*, ed. R. J. Taylor. Upper Saddle River, NJ: Prentice Hall, 79–100.

Bailey, M. (2011). "The Illest": Disability as metaphor in hip hop music. *Blackness and Disability: Critical Examinations and Cultural Interventions*, ed. C. Bell. East Lansing: Michigan State University Press, 141–148.

Barnartt, S. N. (2001). "Using role theory to describe disability." *Research in Social Science and Disability* 2: 53–75.

Barron, K. (1997). "The bumpy road to womanhood." *Disability and Society* 12(2): 223–239.

Bat-Chava, Y. (1994). "Group identification and self-esteem of deaf adults." *Personality and Social Psychology Bulletin* 20: 494–504.

Baxter, C. (1986). *Intellectual Disability: Parental Perceptions and Stigma as Stress.* Unpublished PhD diss., Monash University, Victoria, Australia.

Beart, S., et al. (2005). "How people with intellectual disabilities view their social identity: A review of the literature." *Journal of Applied Research in Intellectual Disabilities* 18: 47–56.

Becker, G. (1980). *Growing Old in Silence: Deaf People in Old Age.* Berkeley: University of California Press.

Becker, H. S. (1963). *Outsiders.* New York: Free Press.

Belgrave, F. Z. (1998). *Psychosocial Aspects of Chronic Illness and Disability Among African Americans.* Westport, CT: Auburn House.

Bell, C., ed. (2011a). *Blackness and Disability: Critical Examinations and Cultural Interventions.* East Lansing: Michigan State University Press.

——— (2011b). Introduction: Doing representational detective work. *Blackness and Disability: Critical Examinations and Cultural Interventions*, ed. C. Bell. East Lansing: Michigan State University Press, 1–7.

Berbrier, M. (2002). "Making minorities: Cultural space, stigma transformation frames, and the categorical status claims of Deaf, gay, and white supremacist activists in late twentieth-century America." *Sociological Forum* 17(4): 553–585.

Bernabeu, E. P. (1958). "The effects of severe crippling on the development of a group of children." *Psychiatry* 21: 169–194.

Bernstein, M. (2005). "Identity politics." *Annual Review of Sociology* 31: 47–74.

Berube, M. (1996). *Life as We Know It: A Father, a Family, and an Exceptional Child.* New York: Vintage.

Birenbaum, A. (1970). "On managing a courtesy stigma." *Journal of Health and Social Behavior* 11: 196–206.

Black, R. S., and L. Prettes (2007). "Victims and victors: Representation of physical disability on the silver screen." *Research and Practice for Persons with Severe Disabilities* 32(1): 66–83.

Blackwell-Stratton, M., et al. (1988). Smashing icons: Disabled women and the disability and women's movements. *Women with Disabilities: Essays in Psychology, Culture, and Politics*, ed. M. Fine and A. Asch. Philadelphia: Temple University Press, 306–332.

Blake, T. R., and J. O. Rust (2002). "Self-esteem and self-efficacy of college students with disabilities." *College Student Journal* 36(2): 214–222.

Block, P., et al. (2002). "Race, poverty and disability: Three strikes and you're out! Or are you?" *Social Policy* 33(1): 34–38.

Blumberg, L. (2004). The virtues of "ballpark normalcy." *Reflections from a Different Journey: What Adults with Disabilities Wish All Parents Knew*, ed. S. D. Klein and J. D. Kemp. New York: McGraw-Hill, 23–26.

Blumer, H. (1962). Society as symbolic interaction. *Human Behavior and Social Processes: An Interactionist Approach*, ed. A. M. Rose. Boston: Houghton Mifflin, 179–192.

Bowker, N., and K. Tuffin (2002). "Disability discourses for online identities." *Disability and Society* 17(3): 327–344.

Brault, M. W. (2012). *Americans with Disabilities: 2010.* Washington, DC: US Census Bureau. www.census.gov.

Britt, L., and D. Heise (2000). From shame to pride in identity politics. *Self, Identity, and Social Movements*, ed. S. Stryker, T. J. Owens, and R. W. White. Minneapolis: University of Minnesota Press.

Brown, J., et al. (2009). "'I am a normal man': A narrative analysis of the accounts of older people with Down's syndrome who lived in institutionalised settings." *British Journal of Learning Disabilities* 38: 217–224.

Browner, C. H., H. M. Preloran, and S. J. Cox. (1999). "Ethnicity, bioethics, and prenatal diagnosis: The amniocentesis decisions of

Mexican-origin women and their partners." *American Journal of Public Health* 89: 1658–1666.

Bruun, F. J. (1995). Hero, beggar, or sports star: Negotiating the identity of the disabled person in Nicaragua. *Disability and Culture*, ed. B. Ingstad and S. R. Whyte. Berkeley: University of California Press, 196–209.

Butler, J. (1990). *Gender Trouble*. London: Routledge, Chapman and Hall.

Cahill, M. A., and M. F. Norden (2003). Hollywood's portrayals of disabled women. *Women, Disability and Identity*, ed. A. Hans and A. Patri. New Delhi: Sage, 56–75.

Carrasquillo, H. (2002). The Puerto Rican family. *Minority Families in the United States: A Multicultural Perspective*, ed. R. J. Taylor. Upper Saddle River, NJ: Prentice Hall, 101–113.

Centers, L., and K. Centers (1963). "A comparison of the body image of amputee and nonamputee children as revealed in figure drawings." *Journal of Projective Techniques and Personality Assessment* 27(June): 158–165.

Cerulo, K. A. (1997). "Identity construction: New issues, new directions." *Annual Review of Sociology* 23: 385–409.

Charlton, J. I. (1998). *Nothing About Us Without Us: Disability Oppression and Empowerment*. Berkeley: University of California Press.

Charmaz, K. (1995). "The body, identity, and self: Adapting to impairment." *Sociological Quarterly* 36(4): 657–680.

——— (1999). "Discoveries" of self in illness. *Health, Illness, and Healing: Society, Social Context, and Self*, ed. K. Charmaz and D. A. Paterniti. Los Angeles: Roxbury Publishing, 72–82.

Chesler, M. (1965). "Ethnocentrism and attitudes toward the physically disabled." *Journal of Personality and Social Psychology* 2: 877–892.

Cloward, R. A., and L. E. Ohlin. (1960). *Delinquency and Opportunity: A Theory of Delinquent Gangs*. New York: Free Press.

Conner, K. O., et al. (2010). "Attitudes and beliefs about mental health among African American older adults suffering from depression." *Journal of Aging Studies* 24(4): 266–277.

Connors, C., and K. Stalker (2007). "Children's experiences of disability: Pointers to a social model of childhood disability." *Disability and Society* 22(1): 19–33.

Cooley, C. H. (1964). *Human Nature and the Social Order*. New York: Schocken Books.

Coppersmith, S. (1967). *The Antecedents of Self-Esteem*. San Francisco: W. H. Freeman.

Cragg, S., and K. Lafreniere (2010). "Effects of Turner syndrome on women's self-esteem and body image." *Journal of Developmental and Physical Disabilities* 22(5): 433–445.

Cummins, R. (2012). Comprehensive Quality of Life Scale. Melbourne: Australia Centre on Quality of Life. www.deakin.edu.au /research/acqol/instruments/comqol-scale/ (accessed January 4, 2012).

Danielson, P. (2004). Disability does not equal liability. *Reflections from a Different Journey: What Adults with Disabilities Wish All Parents Knew*, ed. S. D. Klein and J. D. Kemp. New York: Mc-Graw-Hill, 8–12.

Darling, R. B. (1979). *Families Against Society: A Study of Reactions to Children with Birth Defects*. Beverly Hills, CA: Sage.

——— (1988). "Parental entrepreneurship: A consumerist response to professional dominance." *Journal of Social Issues* 44: 141–158.

——— (1993). "Co-editor's introduction." *Disability Studies Quarterly* 13(4): 1–3.

——— (2000a). *The Partnership Model in Human Services: Sociological Foundations and Practices*. New York: Kluwer/Plenum.

——— (2000b). Stigma of disability. *Encyclopedia of Criminology and Deviant Behavior*, ed. C. D. Bryant. Philadelphia: Brunner-Routledge, 482–485.

——— (2003). "Toward a model of changing disability identities: A proposed typology and research agenda." *Disability and Society* 18: 881–895.

——— (2008). The changing context of neonatal decision making: Are the consumerist and disability rights movements having an effect? *Bioethical Issues, Sociological Perspectives*, ed. B. K. Rothman, E. M. Armstrong, and R. Tiger. Oxford: JAI Press, 65–84.

Darling, R. B., and D. A. Heckert (2010a). "Activism, models, identities, and opportunities: A preliminary test of a typology of disability orientations." *Research in Social Science and Disability* 5: 203–229.

——— (2010b). "Orientations toward disability: Differences over the lifecourse." *International Journal of Disability, Development and Education* 57(2): 131–144.

Davis, F. (1961). "Deviance disavowal: The management of strained interaction by the visibly handicapped." *Social Problems* 9: 120–132.

Deegan, M. J. (1985). A case study of physically disabled women. *Women and Disability: The Double Handicap*, ed. M. J. Deegan and N. A. Brooks. New Brunswick, NJ: Transaction Books, 37–55.

—— (2010). "Feeling normal" and "feeling disabled." *Disability as a Fluid State*, ed. S. N. Barnartt. Bingley, UK: Emerald, 25–48.

DeKlerk, H. M., and L. Ampousah (2003). "The physically disabled woman's experience of self." *Disability and Rehabilitation* 25(19): 1132–1139.

DeVellis, R. F. (1991). *Scale Development: Theory and Application*. Newbury Park, CA: Sage.

Devlieger, P. J. (2010). At the interstices of classification: Notes on the category of disability in sub-Saharan Africa. *Research in Social Science and Disability: Disability as a Fluid State*, ed. S. N. Barnartt. Bingley, UK: Emerald, vol. 5: 69–101.

Devlieger, P., and G. Albrecht (2000). "Your experience is not my experience: The concept and experience of disability on Chicago's Near West Side." *Journal of Disability and Policy Studies* 11: 51–60.

Devlieger, P., et al. (2007). "The production of disability culture among young African-American men." *Social Science and Medicine* 64(9): 1948–1959.

Disability-Research-Discussion-List (2004). disability-research@jisc mail.ac.uk, October 14.

Dobransky, K., and E. Hargittai (2006). "The disability divide in Internet access and use." *Information, Communication and Society* 9(3): 313–334.

Dow, T. E., Jr. (1966). "Optimism, physique, and social class in reaction to disability." *Journal of Health and Social Behavior* 7: 14–19.

Downey, K. J. (1963). "Parental interest in the institutionalized severely mentally retarded child." *Social Problems* 11: 186–193.

Duvdevany, I. (2010). "Self-esteem and perception of quality of life among Israeli women with and without physical disability." *Women and Health* 50(5): 443–458.

Edgerton, R. B. (1993). *The Cloak of Competence*. Berkeley: University of California Press.

Elliot, G. C., et al. (1982). "Understanding Stigma: Dimensions of deviance and coping." *Deviant Behavior* 3(3): 275–300.

Fine, M., and A. Asch (1981). "Disabled women: Sexism without the pedestal." *Journal of Sociology and Social Welfare* 8(2): 233–248.

——— (1988a). "Disability beyond stigma: Social interaction, discrimination, and activism." *Journal of Social Issues* 44(1): 3–22.

——— (1988b). Introduction: Beyond pedestals. *Women with Disabilities: Essays in Psychology, Culture, and Politics*, ed. M. Fine and A. Asch. Philadelphia: Temple University Press, 1–37.

Foster, K., and M. Sandel (2010). "Abuse of women with disabilities: Toward an empowerment perspective." *Sexuality and Disability* 28(3): 177–186.

Freedman, V. A. (2012). "Disability, participation, and subjective well-being among older couples." *Social Science and Medicine* 74(4): 588–596.

Fries, K., ed. (1997). *Staring Back: The Disability Experience from the Inside Out*. New York: Penguin Putnam.

Galvin, R. (2003). "The paradox of disability culture: The need to combine versus the imperative to let go." *Disability and Society* 18(5): 675–690.

Gannotti, M. E., et al. (2001). "Sociocultural influences on disability status in Puerto Rican children." *Physical Therapy* 81(9): 1512–1524.

García-Preto, N. (1982). Puerto Rican families. *Ethnicity and Family Therapy*, ed. M. McGoldrick, J. K. Pearce, and J. Giordano. New York: Guilford Press, 164–186.

Gerschick, T. J. (2000). "Toward a theory of disability and gender." *Signs: Journal of Women in Culture and Society* 25(4): 1263–1268.

Ghali, S. B. (1977). "Culture sensitivity and the Puerto Rican client." *Social Casework* 58: 459–474.

Ghaziani, A. (2004). "Anticipatory and actualized identities: A cultural analysis of the transition from AIDS disability to work." *Sociological Quarterly* 45(2): 273–301.

Giddens, A. (1991). *Modernity and Self-Identity: Self and Society in the Later Modern Age*. Cambridge, UK: Polity Press.

Gill, C. J. (1994). Questioning continuum. *The Ragged Edge: The Disability Experience from the Pages of the First Fifteen Years of the Disability Rag*, ed. B. Shaw. Louisville, KY: Advocado Press.

——— (1997). "Four types of integration in disability identity development." *Journal of Vocational Rehabilitation* 9: 39–46.

Gill, C. J., and W. E. Cross, Jr. (2010). Disability identity and racial-cultural identity development: Points of divergence, convergence, and interplay. *Race, Culture, and Disability: Rehabilitation Science and Practice*, ed. F. E. Balcazar, Y. Suarez-Balcazar, T. Taylor-Ritzler, and C. B. Keys. Sudbury, MA: Jones and Bartlett, 33–52.

Gilson, S. F., and Elizabeth Depoy (2004). "Disability, identity, and cultural diversity." *Review of Disability Studies* 1(1): 16–23.

Glenn, E. N., and S. G. H. Yap (2002). Chinese American families. *Minority Families in the United States: A Multicultural Perspective*, ed. R. J. Taylor. Upper Saddle River, NJ: Prentice Hall, 134–163.

Glenn, S., and C. Cunningham (2001). "Evaluation of self by young people with Down syndrome." *International Journal of Disability, Development and Education* 48(2): 163–177.

Goffman, E. (1958). *The Presentation of Self in Everyday Life*. Edinburgh: University of Edinburgh Social Sciences Research Centre.

——— (1959). *The Presentation of Self in Everyday Life*. Garden City, NY: Doubleday.

——— (1963). *Stigma: Notes on the Management of Spoiled Identity*. Englewood Cliffs, NJ: Prentice Hall.

Gould-Martin, K., and C. Ngin. (1981). Chinese Americans. *Ethnicity and Medical Care*, ed. A. Harwood. Cambridge: Harvard University Press, 130–171.

Graf, N. M., et al. (2007). "Living on the line: Mexican and Mexican American attitudes toward disability." *Rehabilitation Counseling Bulletin* 50(3): 153–165.

Griffin-Shirley, N., and S. L. Nes (2005). "Self-esteem and empathy in sighted and visually impaired preadolescents." *Journal of Visual Impairment and Blindness* 99(5): 276–285.

Groce, N. (2005). Immigrants, disability, and rehabilitation. *Culture and Disability: Providing Culturally Competent Services*, ed. J. H. Stone. Thousand Oaks, CA: Sage, 1–13.

Guttmacher, S., and J. Elinson (1971). "Ethno-religious variation in perceptions of illness." *Social Science and Medicine* 5: 117–125.

Habib, L. A. (1995). "'Women and disability don't mix': Double discrimination and disabled women's rights." *Gender and Development* 3(2): 49–55.

Hahn, H. (1988). "The politics of physical differences: Disability and discrimination." *Journal of Social Issues* 44(1): 39–47.

Hahn, H. D., and T. L. Belt (2004). "Disability identity and attitudes toward cure in a sample of disabled activists." *Journal of Health and Social Behavior* 45: 453–464.

Haller, B., et al. (2006). "Media labeling versus the US disability community identity: A study of shifting cultural language." *Disability and Society* 21(1): 61–75.

Hanna, W. J., and B. Rogovsky (1991). "Women with disabilities: Two handicaps plus." *Disability, Handicap and Society* 6(1): 49–63.

Harrison, A., F. Serafica, and H. McAdoo (1984). Ethnic families of color. *Review of child development research*, ed. R. D. Parke. Chicago: University of Chicago Press, vol. 7: 329–371.

Harry, B. (1992a). *Cultural Diversity, Families, and the Special Education System: Communication and Empowerment.* New York: Teachers College Press.

——— (1992b). "Making sense of disability: Low-income Puerto Rican parents' theories of the problem." *Exceptional Children* 59: 27–40.

Hayward, K. (2009). Creating inclusive disability communities. *Disability and Health Journal* 2.

Higgins, M. (2002). "Disability-Research-Discussion List." disability -research@jiscmail.ac.uk. February 10.

Hockenberry, J. (1995). *Moving Violations, a Memoir: War Zones, Wheelchairs, and Declarations of Independence.* New York: Hyperion.

Hogan, A. (1999). Carving out a space to act: Acquired impairment and contested identity. *Disability Discourse*, ed. M. Corker and S. French. Buckingham: Open University Press, 79–91.

Hogg, M. A., D. J. Terry, and K. M. White (1995). "A tale of two theories: A critical comparison of identity theory with social identity theory." *Social Psychology Quarterly* 58(4): 255–269.

Holt, K. S. (1958). "Home care of severely retarded children." *Pediatrics* 22: 744–755.

Huck, S., et al. (2010). "Self-concept of children with intellectual disability in mainstream settings." *Journal of Intellectual and Developmental Disability* 35(3): 141–164.

Iezzoni, L. I., and E. P. McCarthy et al. (2000). "Mobility problems and perceptions of disability by self-respondents and proxy respondents." *Medical Care* 38: 1051–1057.

Ishii-Kuntz, M. (1997). Japanese American families. *Families in Cultural Context: Strengths and Challenges in Diversity*, ed. M. K. DeGenova. Mountain View, CA: Mayfield Publishing.

Jemta, L., et al. (2009). "Self-esteem in children and adolescents with mobility impairment: Impact on well-being and coping strategies." *Acta Paediatrica* 98(3): 567–572.

Jones, N. L. (2006). *The Americans with Disabilities Act (ADA): The Definition of Disability.* Washington, DC: Congressional Research Service.

Kannen, V. (2008). "Identity treason: Race, disability, queerness, and the ethics of (post)identity practices." *Culture, Theory and Critique* 49(2): 149–163.

Kaplan, H. B., and X. Liu (2000). Social movements as collective coping with spoiled personal identities: Intimations from a panel study of changes in the life course between adolescence and adulthood. *Self, Identity, and Social Movements*, ed. S. Stryker, T. J. Owens, and R. W. White. Minneapolis: University of Minnesota Press, 215–238.

Kelley-Moore, J. A., et al. (2006). "When do older adults become 'disabled'? Social and health antecedents of perceived disability in a panel study of the oldest old." *Journal of Health and Social Behavior* 47: 126–141.

Kent, D. (1988). In search of a heroine: Images of women with disabilities in fiction and drama. *Women with Disabilities: Essays in Psychology, Culture, and Politics*, ed. M. Fine and A. Asch. Philadelphia: Temple University Press, 90–110.

Khoshnood, B., et al. (2006). "Advances in medical technology and creation of disparities: The case of Down syndrome." *American Journal of Public Health* 96(12): 2139–2141.

Kiecolt, K. J. (2000). Self-change in social movements. *Self, Identity, and Social Movements*, ed. S. Stryker, T. J. Owens, and R. W. White. Minneapolis: University of Minnesota Press, 110–131.

Kinch, J. W. (1968). "Experiments in factors related to self-concept change." *Journal of Social Psychology* 74: 251–258.

King, S. V. (1998). "The beam in thine own eye: Disability and the Black church." *Western Journal of Black Studies* 22(1): 37–48.

Kirk, S. (2010). "How children and young people construct and negotiate living with medical technology." *Social Science and Medicine* 71(10): 1796–1803.

Kisor, H. (1990). *What's That Pig Outdoors?* New York: Hill and Wang.

Kuhn, M. H., and T. S. McPartland (1954). "An empirical investigation of self-attitudes." *American Sociological Review* 19: 68–76.

Kuusisto, S. (1998). *Planet of the Blind: A Memoir*. New York: Dial Press.

Landsman, G. H. (1998). "Reconstructing motherhood in the age of 'perfect' babies: Mothers of infants and toddlers with disabilities." *Signs: Journal of Women in Culture and Society* 24(1): 69–99.

Langlois, J. A., S. Haggi et al. (1996). "Self-report of difficulty in performing functional activities indentifies a broad range of disability in old age." *Journal of the American Geriatrics Society* 44: 1421–1428.

Lazerson, M. (1975). Educational institutions and mental subnormality: Notes on writing a history. *The Mentally Retarded and Society: A Social Science Perspective*, ed. M. J. Begab and S. A. Richardson. Baltimore: University Park Press, 33–52.

Lee, E. (1982). A social systems approach to assessment and treatment for Chinese American families. *Ethnicity and Family Therapy*, ed. M. McGoldrick, J. K. Pearce, and J. Giordano. New York: Guilford Press, 527–551.

Lemert, E. M. (1967). *Human Deviance, Social Problems, and Social Control*. Englewood Cliffs, NJ: Prentice-Hall.

Lindgren, K. (2004). Bodies in trouble: Identity, embodiment, and disability. *Gendering Disability*, ed. B. G. Smith and B. Hutchison. New Brunswick, NJ: Rutgers University Press, 145–165.

Link, B. G., et al. (1997). "On stigma and its consequences: Evidence from a longitudinal study of men with dual diagnoses of mental illness and substance abuse." *Journal of Health and Social Behavior* 38(2): 177–190.

Linton, S. (1998). *Claiming Disability: Knowledge and Identity*. New York: New York University Press.

Liu, G. Z. (2005). Best practices: Developing cross-cultural competence from a Chinese perspective. *Culture and Disability: Providing Culturally Competent Services*, ed. J. H. Stone. Thousand Oaks, CA: Sage, 65–86.

Lloyd, M. (1992). "Does she boil eggs? Towards a feminist model of disability." *Disability, Handicap and Society* 7(3): 207–221.

Lofland, J., and R. Stark (1965). "Becoming a world saver: A theory of conversion to a deviant perspective." *American Sociological Review* 30 (December): 862–875.

Longmore, P. K. (2003). *Why I Burned My Book and Other Essays on Disability*. Philadelphia: Temple University Press.

Low, J. (1996). "Negotiating identities, negotiating environments: An interpretation of the experiences of students with disabilities." *Disability and Society* 11(2): 235–248.

Lundgren, D. C. (2004). "Social Feedback and Self-Appraisals: Current Status of the Mead-Cooley Hypothesis." *Symbolic Interaction* 27(2): 267–286.

Mairs, N. (1996). *Waist-High in the World: A Life Among the Nondisabled.* Boston: Beacon Press.

Major, B., and L. T. O'Brien (2005). "The social psychology of stigma." *Annual Review of Psychology* 56: 393–421.

Mansfield, C., et al. (1999). "Termination rates after prenatal diagnosis of Down syndrome, spina bifida, anencephaly, and Turner and Klinefelter syndromes: A systematic literature review." *Prenatal Diagnosis* 19: 808–812.

Martinez, E. A. (1999). Mexican American/Chicano families: Parenting as diverse as the families themselves. *Family Ethnicity: Strength in Diversity*, ed. H. P. McAdoo. Thousand Oaks, CA: Sage: 121–134.

Mary, L. N. (1990). "Reactions of black, Hispanic, and white mothers to having a child with handicaps." *Mental Retardation* 28: 1–5.

Mayer, C. L. (1967). "Relationships of self-concepts and social variables in retarded children." *American Journal of Mental Deficiency* 72: 267–271.

McCall, G. J., and J. L. Simmons (1978). *Identities and Interactions.* New York: Free Press.

McCarthy, H. (2003). "The disability rights movement: Experiences and perspectives of selected leaders in the disability community." *Rehabilitation Counseling Bulletin* 46(4): 209–223.

McDonald, K. E., et al. (2007). "Disability, race/ethnicity and gender: Themes of cultural oppression, acts of individual resistance." *American Journal of Community Psychology* 39: 145–161.

Mead, G. H. (1934). *Mind, Self, and Society.* Chicago: University of Chicago Press.

Meekosha, H. (2002). "Virtual activists? Women and the making of identities of disability." *Hypatia* 17(3): 67–75.

Meissner, A. L., et al. (1967). "Relation of self-concept to impact and obviousness of disability among male and female adolescents." *Perceptual and Motor Skills* 24: 1099–1105.

Mercer, J. R. (1965). "Social system perspective and clinical perspective: Frames of reference for understanding career patterns of persons labeled as mentally retarded." *Social Problems* 13: 18–34.

Merton, R. K. (1949). *Social Theory and Social Structure*. New York: Free Press.

Meyerowitz, J. H. (1962). "Self-derogations in young retardates and special class placement." *Child Development* 33: 443–451.

Middleton, L. (1999). *Disabled Children: Challenging Social Exclusion*. Oxford: Blackwell Science.

Minkler, M., and P. Fadem (2002). "'Successful aging': A disability perspective." *Journal of Disability Policy Studies* 12: 229–235.

Minow, M. (1997). *Not Only for Myself: Identity, Politics, and the Law*. New York: New Press.

Miyahara, M., and J. Piek (2006). "Self-esteem of children and adolescents with physical disabilities: Quantitative evidence from meta-analysis." *Journal of Developmental and Physical Disabilities* 18(3): 219–234.

Moin, V., et al. (2009). "Sexual identity, body image and life satisfaction among women with and without physical disability." *Sexuality and Disability* 27(2): 83–95.

Mpofu, E., and D. A. Harley (2006). "Racial and disability identity: Implications for the career counseling of African Americans with disabilities." *Rehabilitation Counseling Bulletin* 50(1): 14–23.

Murphy, R. F. (1990). *The Body Silent*. New York: W. W. Norton.

Murugami, M. W. (2009). "Disability and identity." *Disability Studies Quarterly* 29(4): 1–4.

Nario-Redmond, M. R. (2010). "Cultural stereotypes of disabled and non-disabled men and women: Consensus for global category representations and diagnostic domains." *British Journal of Social Psychology* 49: 471–488.

Nario-Redmond, M. R., et al. (2011). Redefining disability, reimagining the self: Disability identification predicts strategic responses to stigma and well-being. Unpublished manuscript, Hiram College.

Nash, J. E., and A. Nash (1981). *Deafness in Society*. Lexington, MA: D.C. Heath.

National Organization on Disability (2000). *National Organization on Disability/Harris Survey of Americans with Disabilities*. New York: Harris Interactive.

Newman, J. (1991). Handicapped persons and their families: Philosophical, historical, and legislative perspectives. *The Family with a Handicapped Child*, ed. M. Seligman. Boston: Allyn and Bacon: 1–26.

Nicolaisen, I. (1995). Persons and nonpersons: Disability and person-hood among the Punan Bah of Central Borneo. *Disability and Culture*, ed. B. Ingstad and S. R. Whyte. Berkeley: University of California Press, 38–55.

Niemeier, J. P. (2008). "Unique aspects of women's emotional responses to disability." *Disability and Rehabilitation* 30(3): 166–173.

Nosek, M. A., and R. B. Hughes (2003). "Psychosocial issues of women with physical disabilities: The continuing gender debate." *Rehabilitation Counseling Bulletin* 46(4): 224–234.

Nosek, M. A., et al. (2003). "Self-esteem and women with disabilities." *Social Science and Medicine* 56(8): 1737–1748.

Olin, E., and B. R. Jansson (2009). "On the outskirts of normality: Young adults with disabilities, their belongings and strategies." *International Journal of Qualitative Studies in Health and Well-Being* 4: 256–266.

Oliver, M. (1996). *Understanding Disability: From Theory to Practice*. New York: St. Martin's Press.

Olney, M. F., and K. F. Brockelman (2003). "Out of the disability closet: Strategic use of perception management by select university students with disabilities." *Disability and Society* 18(1): 35–50.

Owens, T. J., and P. J. Aronson (2000). Self-concept as a force in social movement involvement. *Self, Identity, and Social Movements*, ed. S. Stryker, T. J. Owens and R. W. White. Minneapolis: University of Minnesota Press, 191–214.

Paniagua, F. A. (1998). *Assessing and Treating Culturally Diverse Clients: A Practical Guide*. Thousand Oaks, CA: Sage Publications.

Parsons, T. (1951). *The Social System*. New York: Free Press.

Patrick, D. (2012). Perceived Quality of Life Scale. http://depts .washington.edu/yqol/PQOL (accessed January 4, 2012).

Petersen, A. (2006). "An African-American woman with disabilities: The intersection of gender, race, and disability." *Disability and Society* 21(7): 721–734.

Plata, M., and J. Trusty (2005). "Effect of socioeconomic status on general and at-risk high school boys' willingness to accept same-sex peers with LD." *Adolescence* 40(157): 47–66.

Potok, A. (1980). *Ordinary Daylight*. New York: Holt, Rinehart, and Winston.

Preacher, K. J., and R. C. MacCallum (2003). "Repairing Tom

Swift's electric factor analysis machine." *Understanding Statistics* 2: 13–43.

Priestley, M. (1999). Discourse and identity: Disabled children in mainstream high schools. *Disability Discourse*, ed. M. Corker and S. French. Buckingham: Open University Press, 92–102.

Priestley, M., and P. Rabiee (2002). "Older people's organisations and disability issues." *Disability and Society* 17: 597–611.

Putnam, M. (2005). "Developing a framework for political disability identity." *Journal of Disability Policy Studies* 16(3): 188–199.

Rapley, M., et al. (1998). "Invisible to themselves or negotiating identity? The interactional management of 'being intellectually disabled.'" *Disability and Society* 13(5): 807–827.

Richardson, S. A. (1972). "People with cerebral palsy talk for themselves." *Developmental Medicine and Child Neurology* 14: 521–535.

Richardson, S. A., et al. (1961). "Cultural uniformity in reaction to physical disabilities." *American Sociological Review* 26: 241–247.

—— (1964). "Effects of physical disability on a child's description of himself." *Child Development* 35 (September): 893–907.

Rosenberg, M., and R. G. Simmons (1971). *Black and White Self-Esteem: The Urban School Child.* Washington, DC: American Sociological Association.

Rousso, H. (1984). "Fostering healthy self-esteem." *Exceptional Parent* (February): 209–214.

Russell, M. (1994). Malcolm teaches us too. *The Ragged Edge: The Disability Experience from the Pages of the First Fifteen Years of the Disability Rag*, ed. B. Shaw. Louisville, KY: Advocado Press, 11–14.

Safilios-Rothschild, C. (1970). *The Sociology and Social Psychology of Disability and Rehabilitation.* New York: Random House.

Sang, K. K., and C. T. Mowbray (2005). "What affects self-esteem of persons with psychiatric disabilities: The role of causal attributions of mental illnesses." *Psychiatric Rehabilitation Journal* 28(4): 354–361.

Santana-Martin, S. S., and F. O. Santana (2005). An introduction to Mexican culture for service providers. *Culture and Disability: Providing Culturally Competent Services*, ed. J. H. Stone. Thousand Oaks, CA: Sage, 161–186.

Santiago-Rivera, A. L., et al. (2002). *Counseling Latinos and La Familia: A Practical Guide.* Thousand Oaks, CA: Sage.

Scanzoni, J. (1985). Black parental values and expectations of children's occupational and educational success: Theoretical implications. *Black Children: Social, Educational, and Parental environments*, ed. H. P. McAdoo and J. L. McAdoo. Beverly Hills: Sage, 113–122.

Schechter, M. D. (1961). "The orthopedically handicapped child: Emotional reactions." *Archives of General Psychology* 4: 247–253.

Schecter, E. (2012). *Fierce Joy: A Memoir*. New York: Greenpoint Press.

Schneider, J. W., and P. Conrad (1980). "In the closet with illness: Epilepsy, stigma potential, and information control." *Social Problems* 28(1): 32–44.

Schuengel, C., et al. (2006). "Self-worth, perceived competence, and behaviour problems in children with cerebral palsy." *Disability and Rehabilitation* 26(20): 1251–1258.

Schur, L. A. (1998). "Disability and the psychology of political participation." *Journal of Disability Policy Studies* 9(2): 3–31.

——— (2004). Is there still a "double handicap"? Economic, social, and political disparities experienced by women with disabilities. *Gendering Disability*, ed. B. G. Smith and B. Hutchison. New Brunswick, NJ: Rutgers University Press, 253–271.

Scotch, R. (1988). "Disability as the basis for a social movement: Advocacy and the politics of definition." *Journal of Social Issues* 44(1): 159–172.

SDS-Discussion-List (2005). The identity dilemma of hidden disability. SDS_listserv@listserv.uic.edu (posted September 28).

——— (2007). Disability awareness vs. disability pride? SDS_listserv@listserv.uic.edu (posted April 10).

——— (2011). "[SDS] Making its debut appearance in California: The Justin Dart puppet!" Society for Disabled Studies. http://lists.disstudies.org/mailman/listinfo/sds-discuss_lists.disstudies.org (accessed July 9, 2011).

Seligman, M., and R. B. Darling (2007). *Ordinary Families, Special Children: A Systems Approach to Childhood Disability*. New York: Guilford Publications.

Shannon, C. D., et al. (2009). "The effect of contact, context, and social power on undergraduate attitudes toward persons with disabilities." *Journal of Rehabilitation* 75(4): 11–18.

Shapiro, D. R., and J. J. Martin (2010). "Multidimensional physical self-concept of athletes with physical disabilities." *Adapted Physical Activity Quarterly* 27(4): 294–307.

Shapiro, D. R., et al. (2008). "Domain-specific ratings of importance and global self-worth of children with visual impairments." *Journal of Visual Impairment and Blindness* 102(4): 232–244.

Shapiro, J. (1994). *No Pity: People with Disabilities Forging a New Civil Rights Movement.* New York: Times Books.

Shapiro, J., and K. Tittle. (1986). "Psychosocial adjustment of poor Mexican mothers of disabled and nondisabled children." *American Journal of Orthopsychiatry* 56: 289–302.

Sheridan, M. (2001). *Inner Lives of Deaf Children: Interviews and Analysis.* Washington, DC: Gallaudet University Press.

Shibutani, T. (1955). "Reference groups as perspectives." *American Journal of Sociology* 60 (May): 562–569.

——— (1961). *Society and Personality: An Interactionist Approach to Social Psychology.* Englewood Cliffs, NJ: Prentice Hall.

Shon, S. P., and D. Y. Ja. (1982). Asian families. *Ethnicity and Family Therapy,* ed. M. McGoldrick, J. K. Pearce, and J. Giordano. New York: Guilford Press, 208–228.

Siebers, T. (2006). Disability studies and the future of identity politics. *Identity Politics Reconsidered,* ed. L. M. Alcoff, M. Hames-Garcia, S. P. Mohanty, and P. M. I. Moya. New York: Palgrave Macmillan, 10–29.

Silverstein, A. B., and H. A. Robinson (1956). "The representation of orthopedic disability in children's figure drawings." *Journal of Consulting Psychology* 20 (October): 333–341.

Smart, J. F., and D. W. Smart (1991). "Acceptance of disability and the Mexican American culture." *Rehabilitation Counseling Bulletin* 34(4): 357–368.

Smits, S. J. (1964). "Reactions of self and others to the obviousness and severity of physical disability." *Dissertation Abstracts International* 25(1–3): 1324–1325.

Snow, D. A., and L. Anderson (1987). "Identity work among the homeless: The verbal construction and avowal of personal identities." *American Journal of Sociology* 92: 1336–1371.

Snow, D. A., and D. McAdam (2000). Identity work processes in the context of social movements: Clarifying the identity/movement nexus. *Self, Identity, and Social Movements,* ed. S. Stryker, T. J. Owens, and R. W. White. Minneapolis: University of Minnesota Press, 41–67.

Soyupek, F., et al. (2010). "Do the self-concept and quality of life decrease in CP patients? Focusing on the predictors of self-concept and quality of life." *Disability and Rehabilitation* 32(13): 1109–1115.

Stets, J. E., and P. J. Burke (2000). "Identity theory and social identity theory." *Social Psychology Quarterly* 63(3): 224–237.

Strauss, A. (1962). Transformations of identity. *Human Behavior and Social Processes*, ed. A. M. Rose. Boston: Houghton Mifflin, 63–85.

Stryker, S., and P. J. Burke (2000). "The past, present, and future of an identity theory." *Social Psychology Quarterly* 63(4): 284–297.

Stuart, O. W. (1992). "Race and disability: Just a double oppression?" *Disability, Handicap and Society* 7(2): 177–188.

Sullivan, H. S. (1947). The human organism and its necessary environment. *Conceptions of Modern Psychiatry*, ed. H. S. Sullivan. Washington, DC: William Alanson White Psychiatric Foundation, 14–27.

Swain, J., and C. Cameron (1999). Unless otherwise stated: Discourses of labelling and identity in coming out. *Disability Discourse*, ed. M. Corker and S. French. Buckingham, UK: Open University Press, 68–78.

Swain, J., and S. French (2000). "Towards an affirmation model of disability." *Disability and Society* 15: 569–582.

Sze, S., and S. Valentin (2007). "Self-concept and children with disabilities." *Education* 127(4): 552–557.

Terhune, P. S. (2005). "African-American developmental disability discourses: Implications for policy development." *Journal of Policy and Practice in Intellectual Disabilities* 2(1): 18–28.

Thomas, C. (1999a). *Female Forms: Experiencing and Understanding Disability*. Buckingham, UK: Open University Press.

——— (1999b). Narrative identity and the disabled self. *Disability Discourse*, ed. M. F. Corker, and S. French. Buckingham, UK: Open University Press.

Thomas, W. I. (1928). *The Child in America: Behavior Problems and Programs*. New York: Alfred A. Knopf.

Toch, H. (1965). *The Social Psychology of Social Movements*. Indianapolis: Bobbs-Merrill.

Tollifson, J. (1997). Imperfection is a beautiful thing: On disability and meditation. *Staring Back: The Disability Experience from the Inside Out*, ed. K. Fries. New York: Plume.

Towler, A. J., and D. J. Schneider (2005). "Distinctions among stigmatized groups." *Journal of Applied Social Psychology* 35(1): 1–14.

US Bureau of Justice Statistics (2011). *Crimes Against Persons with Disabilities, 2008–2010 Statistical Tables.* http://bjs.gov/index .cfm?ty=pbdetail+iid=2238 (accessed December 12, 2011).

US Bureau of Labor Statistics (2011) *Persons with a Disability: Labor Force Characteristics Summary*, 1–3. http://data.bls.gov /cgi-bin/print.pl/news.release/disabl.nro.htm (accessed December 12, 2011).

US Bureau of the Census (2012). Americans with Disabilities: 2010. Washington, DC. www.census.gov/prod/2012pubs/p70-131.pdf (accessed December 7, 2012).

Verbrugge, L. M., and L.-S. Yang (2002). "Aging with disability and disability with aging." *Journal of Disability Policy Studies* 12(4): 253–267.

Vernon, A. (1999). "The dialectics of multiple identities and the disabled people's movement." *Disability and Society* 14(3): 385–398.

Voysey, M. (1975). *A Constant Burden: The Reconstitution of Family Life.* London: Routledge and Kegan Paul.

Watson, N. (2002). "Well, I know this is going to sound very strange to you, but I don't see myself as a disabled person: Identity and disability." *Disability and Society* 17(5): 509–527.

Westbrook, M. T., et al. (1993). "Attitudes towards disabilities in a multicultural society." *Social Science and Medicine* 36(5): 615–623.

Whitney, C. (2006). "Intersections in identity—identity development among queer women with disabilities." *Sexuality and Disability* 24(1): 39–53.

Whittington-Walsh, F. (2002). "From freaks to savants: Disability and hegemony from *The Hunchback of Notre Dame* (1939) to *Sling Blade* (1997)." *Disability and Society* 17(6): 695–707.

Willie, C. V. R., and R. J. Reddick (2003). *A New Look at Black Families.* Walnut Creek, CA: Altamira Press.

Wilson, D. J. (2004). Fighting polio like a man: Intersections of masculinity, disability, and aging. *Gendering Disability*, ed. B. G. Smith and B. Hutchison. New Brunswick, NJ: Rutgers University Press, 119–133.

Wolfensberger, W. (1972). *Normalization: The Principle of Normalization in Human Services.* Toronto: National Institute on Mental Retardation.

——— (1995). "An 'if this, then that' formulation of decisions related to social role valorization as a better way of interpreting it to people." *Mental Retardation* 33(3): 163–169.

World Health Organization (1999). International Classification of Functioning, Disability and Health. 2nd ed. Geneva: World Health Organization.

Wright, B. A. (1983). *Physical disability: A psychosocial approach.* New York: Harper and Row.

Wylie, R. C. (1974). *The Self Concept: A Review of Methodological Considerations and Measuring Instruments.* Lincoln: University of Nebraska Press.

Wysocki, B. A., and E. Whitney (1965). "Body image of crippled children as seen in draw-a-person test behavior." *Perceptual and Motor Skills* 21: 499–504.

Yee, L. Y. (1988). "Asian children." *Teaching Exceptional Children* 20(4): 49–50.

Zitzelsberger, H. (2005). "(In)visibility: Accounts of embodiment of women with physical disabilities and differences." *Disability and Society* 20(4): 389–403.

Zunich, M., and B. E. Ledwith (1965). "Self-concepts of visually handicapped and sighted children." *Perceptual and Motor Skills* 21: 771–774.

Index

Books in the Series

About the Book

Rosalyn Darling offers a sweeping examination of disability and identity, parsing the shifting forces that have shaped individual and societal understandings of ability and impairment across time.

Darling focuses on the relationship between societal views and the self-conceptions of people with mental and physical impairments. She also illuminates the impact of the disability rights movement, life-course dynamics, and race and gender in creating a diversity of disability identities. Her seminal work reveals the remarkable resilience of individuals in the face of profound social and material barriers, at the same time that it enhances our understanding of the construction and experience of "difference" in our changing society.

Rosalyn Benjamin Darling is professor emeritus of sociology at Indiana University of Pennsylvania and visiting professor of sociology at the University of North Carolina–Chapel Hill.